Hear, My Son
An Examination of the
Fatherhood of Yahweh
in Deuteronomy

Ralph Allan Smith

Hear, My Son:
An Examination of the Fatherhood of Yahweh in Deuteronomy
Copyright © 2011 Athanasius Press
205 Roselawn
Monroe, Louisiana 71201
www.athanasiuspress.org

All rights reserved. No part of this publication may be reproduced, stored in a retrieval system, or transmitted in any form or by any means—electronic, mechanical, photocopy, recording, or any other—except for brief quotations in printed reviews, without the prior permission of the publisher.

This book is dedicated to my friends and mentors

James B. Jordan and Peter J. Leithart

*with sincere gratitude for many years
of fellowship in Christ and the work for His kingdom.*

Table of Contents

Foreword	i
Introduction	iii
Chapter One *Explicit Statements of Father/son Relationship*	9
Chapter Two *The Double Promise of the Fifth Word*	25
Chapter Three *A Single Promise from the Fifth Word*	41
Chapter Four *The Rebellious Son*	65
Chapter Five *The Covenant of the Father and the Son*	89
Conclusion	107
Appendix I	109
Appendix II	117

Foreword

This study of Deuteronomy is part of my preliminary work on a commentary for Athanasius Press. I decided to publish this essay as a separate work in order to be able to put into print technical material which would not fit well into the commentary itself. This also gives me the opportunity to express my gratitude to Athanasius Press and other friends in the CREC who have made my publishing possible and who have helped our church in Japan by prayers and donations.

It was originally through the kindness of Doug Wilson and Christ Church, Moscow, Idaho, that my family and our church came to know of the CREC. Christ Church provided generous help for us during a crisis, even though they hardly knew us. Another branch of Christ Church's ministry, Canon Press, kindly published three of my books.

Both through Covenant Media Foundation and with Grace Covenant Church, Randy Booth has provided concrete aid for our ministry in Japan for many years. I am also grateful to the many other CREC pastors and churches who have prayed for us and donated to the ministry in Japan.

Garry Vanderveen and Christ Covenant Church in Langley, British Colombia took on the burden of being our sponsor church and they have supported us generously in prayer and gifts.

I also want to express special thanks to Vic Martens who proofread the text for me and saved me from many embarrassing mistakes.

Introduction

The book of Deuteronomy is quintessential Biblical law. Written by Moses at the end of his life as his final testimony to the people he had been leading for forty years, Deuteronomy was the constitution for ancient Israel. It provided the new perspectives on the Law that would be needed as Israel took up residence in the Promised Land. The laws in Exodus, Leviticus, and Numbers did not address certain issues and many laws needed to be restated to fit the situation Israel would face in the land of Canaan.

It is commonly thought that when a priest in Josiah's day was said to have found "the book of the law of Yahweh given by Moses" (2 Chr. 34:14), the reference was to Deuteronomy. It is also commonly understood that the history of Israel from Joshua to Kings is written from the perspective of the laws, blessings, and curses of Deuteronomy and that the prophets' warnings of the curses impending on Israel and Judah rely heavily on Deuteronomy. Most remarkable is our Lord's use of Deuteronomy when tempted by the Devil in the wilderness, for Jesus answered Satan with Scriptural quotations exclusively derived from Deuteronomy 6–8. It would be hard, therefore, to overestimate the importance of understanding Deuteronomy for our understanding of the Bible. It is one of the must crucial of books.

However, for many modern Christians, Deuteronomy is seen as either too difficult to understand or too far from the concerns of our day—it is ancient law, outdated and no longer able to address the complex issues of a modern society. Furthermore, Deuteronomy is "law"—that from which we in the age of grace have been delivered. Law hangs over us the sign of our condemnation and cries out for our death. But now that we are saved by grace, we are no longer under the awful law with its strict rules and condemnation.

There are many problems with this sort of an approach, whether in the context of dispensational theology or of a reformed theology such as Meredith Kline's. Both the dispensational view and Kline's view underststand law and grace as different "dispensations" and place them in stark contrast. Not only do these views of the Law undermine our reading and understanding of Deuteronomy, they distort our whole understanding of Biblical covenantal revelation.[1]

A right reading of Deuteronomy opens up this book of law as a book of loving instruction from a Father who desperately seeks the blessing of His wayward son. The key to understanding Deuteronomy is found in the repeated references to Yahweh as Israel's father and the abundant allusions to the promises of the Fifth Word. The allusions clearly testify that if Israel will love and obey Yahweh, he will be blessed as Yahweh's obedient son. תּוֹרָה (torah), therefore, should not be understood as "law," but usually as "instruction." Even the commandments, precepts, and judgments of the books of Moses,

---

1. For a fuller statement of Kline's view and the problems it creates, see my *Eternal Covenant: How the Trinity Reshapes Covenant Theology* (Moscow, ID: Canon Press, 2003).

many of which have direct social and political implications, should be understood in the light of the larger covenantal picture.

Certainly Yahweh is Israel's King and Lord (Deut. 33:3–5). The various and sundry rules for life He lays down are to be obeyed and He is to be honored. But Israel is not primarily depicted as a vassal,[2] even when Israel is called "servant." Rather, the metaphor applied by Scripture, beginning with the Exodus, is sonship (Ex. 4:22).[3] Thus, if Yahweh is King, Israel is His prince, the son of the Great King over all. If this metaphor underlies the whole instruction of Deuteronomy, rather than being similar to the codes of Hammurabi or Ur-Nammu, Deuteronomy is much more like Proverbs, where Solomon offers instruction for his beloved son.

That is my thesis in this book: the Law given to Israel at Mt. Sinai and restated by Moses almost forty years later just before he died is the loving instruction of Father Yahweh for His son, the nation of Israel—His

---

2. Contra Meredith Kline's thesis in *The Treaty of the Great King* (Grand Rapids: Eerdmans, 1963). Kline views God's covenant with Israel primarily through the lens of the Ancient Near Eastern treaty. As I argue in chapter five, if we take Biblical chronology seriously, the Ancient Near Eastern treaty forms are dependent on the influence of Noah. Covenants and related forms had their beginning with the Creator God. Historical critical studies that attempt to place the Bible within the Ancient Near Eastern context work in the wrong direction. It is the history, politics, and religion of the Ancient Near East that needs to be located in the Biblical context.

3. My use of the word "metaphor" and similar expressions is not intended to suggest that language like "firstborn" is just a literary picture with no corresponding reality, as if Moses used this language for effect. According to the Bible, man was created as God's "image," so that man himself is the highest symbol in a creation that is entirely symbolic and revelatory. In such a world, "metaphor" is essence, not mere window dressing.

treasured possession and the royal priesthood. I appeal to three lines of argument to support my contention that the Father/son metaphor is basic to our understanding of Deuteronomy.

First, I draw attention to explicit statements of Yahweh's fatherhood in Deuteronomy. The exact expression used in Exodus 4:22, בְּנִי בְכֹרִי יִשְׂרָאֵל, "Israel is My firstborn son," is not repeated in Deuteronomy. But there are various expressions which forthrightly express the Father/son relationship in no uncertain terms, even though they are relatively few.

Second, I show how allusions to the promises of the Fifth Word pervade Deuteronomy. What was promised to children in the home for honoring their fathers and mothers is promised over and over to the people of Israel if they would honor their Father Yahweh. More than anything else Deuteronomy's recurring Fifth Word refrain insinuates the Father/son image into the minds of the reader, impressing it on the heart of those who have ears to hear. The Father/son metaphor so permeates Deuteronomy that it becomes the dominating covenantal image. The Torah of Moses is the Torah that Father Yahweh gave to His beloved son Israel.

Third, I point out another allusion in Deuteronomy that adds to the emphasis on the Father/son metaphor, but also alters one aspect of the picture significantly. Though on the one hand, Deuteronomy constantly depicts Yahweh as a loving Father, Israel, on the other hand, is just as consistently depicted as a foolish and rebellious son, like the son in Deuteronomy 21:18–21 (in the law of the rebellious son), who is sentenced to death.

Both by direct statement and by metaphor, Deuteronomy keeps before us the image of Yahweh as loving Father. Less emphasized, but sufficiently clear is the picture of Israel as a foolish and disobedient son, who cannot be cured of his intransigence. However, death is not the end. Deuteronomy offers hope for the future with the promise of a resurrection of the nation and the gift of a new heart (Deut. 30:6; cf. 32:36–43), a promise Jeremiah and Ezekiel put into their prophecy of a new covenant to come.

I argue further that that the Father/son metaphor for the covenantal relationship between Yahweh and Israel is not based upon a covenant idea invented by Ancient Near Eastern societies, borrowed by God and Moses, and perpetuated because of its use in Scripture. "Covenant" is not a relic of the past that we can and perhaps should set aside for some more modern and up-to-date metaphor. Rather, the covenant idea found in Scripture is grounded in the reality of the covenantal relationship of the Father, Son, and Spirit. The Biblical covenant is not an Ancient Near Eastern convention; it is a description of how Father, Son, and Spirit relate to one another from all eternity and of how the Triune God relates to His creation from the beginning until forever.

Chapter One

Explicit Statements of Father/son Relationship

The unique and unrepeated declaration in the book of Exodus that Israel is Yahweh's firstborn son (Ex. 4:22–23)[1] stands out in the Exodus story because of its defining place at the very beginning. It is foundational for all that follows, especially the climactic judgment on Egypt, the death of the firstborn sons of the land. Though the language is not repeated in the book of Exodus, the idea of Israel as God's firstborn son obviously determines the entire history that follows.[2] This comes to expression in key passages in the book of Deu-

---

1. Jeremiah 31:9 alludes to the Exodus story and the identification of Israel as Yahweh's firstborn: "For I am a father to Israel, and Ephraim is My firstborn." But here Israel is distinguished from Judah, and Ephraim is put forth as representative for the whole of the northern tribes.

2. The Gospel of John, for example, introduces Jesus as the "logos," but it does not repeat that word or make "logos" into a regularly used title for Christ. All the same, we cannot rightly read the Gospel of John without the words of the prologue haunting us to the end.

teronomy, where we find the Father/son relationship between Yahweh and Israel explicitly stated. I intend to show that the initial paradigm presented in Exodus 4:22 is determinative and that Deuteronomy shows clearly that the Father/son metaphor is fundamental to Israel's covenant with Yahweh, defining its very essence.

What we shall see in the chapters that follow is that explicit references to Yahweh as Israel's Father in Deuteronomy are emphasized by two sets of allusions. The first is to the Fifth Word. Deuteronomy contains numerous allusions to the promises of the Fifth Word, which show the concrete implications of the explicit statements to the Israelites that their relationship with Yahweh was a Father/son relationship. If the children of Israel will honor their Heavenly Father, they will live long in the land and prosper, for the Father delights to bless His son.

The second set of allusions complicates the picture, for these passages point to the law in Deuteronomy about the incorrigible son (Deut. 21:18–21). When a grown-up son refuses to listen to or obey his parents, becomes a drunkard and a glutton, and his parents lose all control over him, there comes a point at which they might bring him to the elders of the city and call for judgment against him. Remarkably, the same language that describes the disobedient son is also used to describe the children of Israel. The analogy is clear and Deuteronomy makes it central to our understanding of Yahweh and Israel. Though Yahweh loves the children of Israel, both collectively and individually, as His dear children, He knows their hearts. They are a nation of rebellious sons, for whom the only "hope" is judgment and, then, life in the resurrected condition (cf. Deut. 29–30).

These two sets of allusions are grounded in the explicit references to Yahweh as Israel's Father in four crucial passages that link the beginning, middle, and end of the book of Deuteronomy. These references, reinforced by the allusions, define the book of Deuteronomy as the Father's loving instruction to His wayward son. The analogy stretches backward to Eden and the typology points forward to the prodigal son as an image of the wayward nation.

The first statement of the Father/son relationship in Deuteronomy stands out not only because of its place near the beginning of the book but also because it is among the most tender and gracious representations of Yahweh's fatherly care (Deut. 1:31). Even more important, it occurs in a context which describes the rebellion of the children of Israel against Yahweh, significantly setting before us a paradigmatic metaphor that echoes throughout the rest of the book. The second statement occurs in the exposition of the First Word[3] in a passage that sets forth Yahweh's fatherly love during the forty years in the wilderness (Deut. 8:5). The third statement occurs at the very beginning of the exposition of the Third Word and is parallel to the expressions "holy people" and "treasured possession" (Deut. 14:1-2), and, in distinction from the first two references, does not refer to what Yahweh had done in the past, but how Israel was to live after she entered the Promised Land. The fourth statement, or set of statements, occurs in one of the most important sections of the book of Deuteronomy, the Song of Moses (Deut. 32:5-6, 18-20). Though the key words from 21:18-21 describing the re-

---

3. See James B. Jordan, *Covenant Sequence in Leviticus and Deuteronomy* (Tyler, TX: Institute for Christian Economics, 1989). Jordan outlines Deuteronomy 6–26 as an exposition of the Ten Words in order. Walter Kaiser, following Stephen A. Kaufmann, offers a similar analysis in *Toward an Old Testament Ethics* (Grand Rapids: Zondervan, 1983), 127–37.

bellious son do not appear, the description of Israel as perverse, unfaithful, crooked, twisted, blemished, and foolish certainly counts as parallel to the expression "stubborn and rebellious," especially since the paradigm has been established earlier. Moreover, the song is introduced in Deuteronomy 31:24–29 as part of the witness against the children of Israel that they have been "rebellious and stubborn" (31:27).

Each of these statements deserves at least brief consideration in context. Keep in mind, however, that in Moses' original sermon, these direct assertions of Yahweh's fatherhood are interspersed with numerous allusions to the Fifth Word and the law of the unruly son.

Deuteronomy 1:31

Early in Deuteronomy, God's tender care as Israel's father is expressed in language that sets the stage for the rest of the book.

> Yahweh your God who goeth before you, he will fight for you, according to all that he did for you in Egypt before your eyes, and in the wilderness, where thou hast seen how that Yahweh thy God bare thee, as a man doth bear his son, in all the way that ye went, until ye came unto this place. (1:30–31)

The statement that "Yahweh thy God bare thee" connects with Moses' words in verse 9 and in verse 12: "I am not able to bear . . ." and "How can I myself alone bear . . ." The burden of leading Israel was more than Moses could handle, but Yahweh bore the children of Israel as a Father carries a little child.[4] Thus, at the very

---

4. Similar expressions are used in Exodus 19:4, where God says, "I bore you on eagles' wings" and in Deuteronomy 32:11, where God is pictured as an eagle carrying Israel on its wings. The

beginning of the book of Deuteronomy, a threefold reference to bearing and a contrast between Moses' inability and Yahweh's sufficiency—demonstrated by His powerful defeat of the enemies and protection in the wilderness—highlights Yahweh's gracious care for His people.

The context in which this remarkable statement occurs brings out the deep contrast between Yahweh's kind care and Israel's stubborn rebellion. In the larger paragraph, Moses is reminding the children of Israel of their climactic act of apostasy and unbelief at Kadesh-barnea (Deut. 1:19–33). As a rebellious son, they refused to follow Moses into the Promised Land and determined instead to appoint a new leader to take them back to Egypt (Num. 14:4). The statement of God's love and care for Israel was part of Moses' attempt to persuade them to trust Him and follow Him into the land of Canaan. Moses reminded Israel that in the Exodus God "carried" them like a man "carries" his son from Egypt to Sinai—in other words, the Father's grace had brought the rebellious son to where he was.

Thus, when the statement of the Father/son metaphor first appears in Deuteronomy, the Father's tender care for His son—"Yahweh thy God did bare thee, as a man bares his son"—is specifically set against the unbelief and rebellion of Israel.[5]

---

metaphor in Exodus, as in Deuteronomy 32:11, is of a mother's tender love for her children. Considering the significance of the passage in which this initially occurs, we have to say that the mother/son analogy is also prominent theologically, even if it does not appear often. The same Hebrew word for "bear" (נשׂא) is used in Deuteronomy 1:31, 32:11, and Exodus 19:4.

5. Note that 1:43 is the first occurrence in Deuteronomy of the important expression לֹא שָׁמַע, one of the characteristics of the rebellious son in Deuteronomy 21:18–21. It is sometimes translated "would not listen" and other times "would not obey"

Yet ye would not go up, but rebelled against the commandment of Yahweh your God ... (1:26)

Yet in this thing ye did not believe Yahweh your God ... (1:32)

So I spake unto you, and ye hearkened not; but ye rebelled against the commandment of Yahweh, and were presumptuous, and went up into the hill-country. (1:43)

Israel is the son whom the Father carried in His arms from Egypt to Kadesh-barnea, but who responded in unbelief, a rebellious son who grew up to be worthless. The allusion to Israel's determination to reject Yahweh and Moses points to the narrative in Numbers 14, where the statement "Let us make a captain, and let us return to Egypt" (Num 14:4) constitutes decisive rejection of the Abrahamic covenant, the Promised Land, and the special favor shown to the children of Israel at

---

(Deut. 1:43; 8:20; 9:23; 11:28; 18:19; 21:18; 28:45, 62; 30:17). Daniel J. Elezar argues that "hearken" is the best translation, in spite of it being somewhat old English. "Hearken is an archaism in English, featured in the King James translation of the Bible, hence shamoa is sometimes translated as 'obey' in more modern English versions of Scripture. But they are not the same at all and abandonment of the older word represents the abandonment of a critical biblical concept that change [sic] the whole meaning of the text and the whole biblical understanding of how humans act. To hearken is very different than to obey. Hearkening is an active form of consent whereby the individual receives an instruction by hearing it and in the process of hearkening makes a decision to follow it. The act of hearkening is an act of hearing, considering, agreeing, and then acting. It is a sign of human freedom—of free will—whereby in order to act humans must consciously decide to do so, even in response to God." in "Deuteronomy as Israel's Ancient Constitution: Some Preliminary Reflections," online at https://secured4.catom.com/JCPA/dje/articles2/deut-const.htm

Sinai where Yahweh declared them to be His treasure, chosen from all the nations of the world (Ex. 19:5–6). The first generation rejected the love and blessing that was graciously bestowed upon them for the sake of Abraham, so they had to die in the wilderness because of their own sins. They also died as a lesson to generations to come, to teach them the fear of Yahweh. But the sad reality that Yahweh told Moses was that in spite of the wilderness lessons, even the generations to come would be disobedient sons (Deut. 31:16–18).

The basic paradigm for the whole book is set out in the very beginning of Deuteronomy. Both Yahweh's fatherly care and Israel's rebellious heart appear in the very first paragraph of the book where Moses recites the history of the Exodus generation.

Deuteronomy 8:5

The next explicit reference to the Father/son relationship between God and Israel is in Deuteronomy 8:5. Chapter 8 in Deuteronomy is part of Moses' application of the First Word (Deut. 6–11) and an important passage that Jesus quoted when repelling the Devil's temptation (Matt. 4:1–4). If we had no other reason for regarding this paragraph as important, Jesus' use of it would certify its significance to us.

Whereas the first reference spoke of Yahweh as carrying the sons of Israel as a man carries a child, the second reference is to discipline, child training.

> And thou shalt consider in thy heart, that, as a man chasteneth his son, so Yahweh thy God chasteneth[6] thee. (8:5)

---

6. The Hebrew word for discipline in Deuteronomy (יִסַּר) alludes not only to the Father/son relationship in general but spe-

These words summarize Yahweh's dealing with the children of Israel throughout the 40 years of wandering, as the previous context makes clear.

> And thou shalt remember all the way which Yahweh thy God hath led thee these forty years in the wilderness, that he might humble thee, to prove thee, to know what was in thy heart, whether thou wouldest keep his commandments, or not. And he humbled thee, and suffered thee to hunger, and fed thee with manna, which thou knewest not, neither did thy fathers know; that he might make thee know that man doth not live by bread only, but by every word that proceedeth out of the mouth of Yahweh doth man live. Thy raiment waxed not old upon thee, neither did thy foot swell, these forty years. (Deut. 8:2-4)

For forty years Yahweh disciplined the children of Israel so that they would learn what Adam was supposed to have understood in the Garden—man lives by the Word of God.[7] The discipline of the wilderness wandering was intended to teach them to trust Yahweh and His word, so that when they came into the land of Canaan, they would be trained to follow Him. Yahweh's discipline was the instruction of fatherly love. After stating this, Moses continues in Deuteronomy 8:6 to teach the children of Israel the correct response to the wilderness training.

---

cifically to the case of the disobedient son. It occurs only four times (Deut 4:36; 8:5; 21:18).

7. The Hebrew text says literally, "all that proceeds from the mouth of Yahweh" but the Septuagint (LXX) translates this "every word that proceeds." Jesus quoted the LXX, suggesting that the translation expressed the spirit and essence of the original.

> Therefore thou shalt keep the commandments of Yahweh thy God, to walk in his ways,[8] and to fear him. (Deut. 8:6)

It is also noteworthy that from the reference to Yahweh as Father in chapter 1 to the next reference in chapter 8, there is historical progress in the time period being referred to. The initial reference covered the time from the Exodus to the arrival at Kadesh-barnea, the first two years after the Exodus. In Deuteronomy 8:5, this same fatherly love characterizes the entire period of wilder-

---

8. The expression "to walk in his ways" should be understood, I believe, in terms of the Father/son metaphor. The good Father set an example for His sons, showing them how to live in the world. To imitate Him is the essence of Israel's righteousness, so the whole Law can be summed up in the words "Ye shall be holy, for I am holy" (in various forms: Leviticus 11:44-45; 19:2; 20:26). In Deuteronomy, walking in His ways is made parallel to keeping His commandments, but the commandments are instruction for Yahweh's children to imitate Him and His ways. Joseph Ozarowski writes, "Thus in Jewish eyes, we can deduce from the above passages that the one who truly wishes to walk in the path of God must imitate God. Specifically, this refers to *hesed*, lovingkindness, at the crisis points in life such as illness and death. By comforting the bereaved and cheering the ill, we follow 'God's path,' acting as God does." Joseph S. Ozarowski, *To Walk in God's Ways: Jewish Pastoral Perspectives on Illness and Bereavement* (Lanham, MD: Rowman and Littlefield, 2004), 4. In this context, the other expressions, too—"keep the commandments of Yahweh thy God," and "fear him"—should also be interpreted in the light of the Father/son metaphor. Also, contrary to those who speak of Deuteronomy as having elements of wisdom literature, we ought to think of the relationship the other way around. Moses wrote the Law long before Solomon. But Solomon rightly understood that the imitation of Yahweh Himself was the aim of the Law, so, borrowing from Deuteronomy, he imitated Yahweh in providing Torah (Prov. 1:8; 3:1; 4:2; 6:20, 23; 7:2), commandments (Prov. 2:1; 3:1; 4:4; 6:20, 23; 7:1-2), and discipline (Prov. 19:18; 29:17; 31:1) for his son.

ness wandering. In other words, even though at Kadesh-barnea His son had rejected Him in unbelief and decided to leave Yahweh to return to Egypt, Yahweh did not forsake His son, but instead disciplined him with a Father's gracious love. Of course, the judgment on the first generation was not final rejection of the children of Israel as a nation. It was not even necessarily final rejection of the first generation, since Yahweh fed them and preserved them during the entire wilderness era. For forty years, Yahweh fed his disobedient son with manna, preserved his clothing and took care of him along the way, so that he could learn the essential lesson of the covenant: "that man doth not live by bread only, but by every word that proceedeth out of the mouth of Yahweh doth man live" (8:3b).

This is followed, however, by a warning, the essence of which is to urge Israel not to forget Yahweh and turn away from Him. In other words, Moses urges the next generations not to be rebellious sons that bring upon themselves the punishment of death.

> Beware lest thou forget Yahweh thy God, in not keeping his commandments, and his ordinances, and his statutes, which I command thee this day: lest, when thou hast eaten and art full, and hast built goodly houses, and dwelt therein; and when thy herds and thy flocks multiply, and thy silver and thy gold is multiplied, and all that thou hast is multiplied; then thy heart be lifted up, and thou forget Yahweh thy God, who brought thee forth out of the land of Egypt, out of the house of bondage; who led thee through the great and terrible wilderness, wherein were fiery serpents and scorpions, and thirsty ground where was no water; who brought thee forth water out of the rock of flint; who fed thee in the wilderness with manna, which thy fa-

thers knew not; that he might humble thee, and that he might prove thee, to do thee good at thy latter end: and lest thou say in thy heart, My power and the might of my hand hath gotten me this wealth. But thou shalt remember Yahweh thy God, for it is he that giveth thee power to get wealth; that he may establish his covenant which he sware unto thy fathers, as at this day. And it shall be, if thou shalt forget Yahweh thy God, and walk after other gods, and serve them, and worship them, I testify against you this day that ye shall surely perish. As the nations that Yahweh maketh to perish before you, so shall ye perish; because ye would not hearken unto the voice of Yahweh your God. (8:11–20)

Deuteronomy 14:21

The next explicit reference to God's fatherhood describes the nation as God's sons, plural, and makes this fact the basis for ethical stipulation.

Ye are the sons of Yahweh your God: ye shall not cut yourselves, nor make any baldness between your eyes for the dead. For thou art a holy people unto Yahweh thy God, and Yahweh hath chosen thee to be a people for his own possession, above all peoples that are upon the face of the earth. (14:1–2)

Note that the command to the individual members of the nation—"ye are," "ye shall not"—is immediately followed by language that addresses the nation as a whole ("thou art")—"For thou art a holy people unto Yahweh."[9] Thus, both as a nation and as individual members of the nation, the children of Israel were taught to think of Yahweh as their heavenly Father. They were

---

9. Note that עַם קָדוֹשׁ is a distinctly Deuteronomic phrase (Deut. 7:6; 14:2, 21; 26:19; 28:9).

also taught that being members of the family of a holy God meant that they were required to imitate His holiness. This context makes clear what was implicit from the book of Exodus (19:5–6), to which this verse alludes through the use of the rare word סְגֻלָּה (possession).[10] Choosing Israel as a holy nation and a people for His own possession is equivalent to publicly declaring Israel to be the firstborn son of Yahweh. The expressions overlap; they all describe Israel's profoundly special privilege. The allusion to Exodus makes this seemingly unimportant passage—a command about mourning ceremonies—profoundly significant for our basic understanding of Yahweh's relationship with His precious people.

Note also the nature of the ethical instruction here. Moses insists that to be a son is to be blessed with a privilege that brings with it ethical obligations in all of life. Thus Moses offers ethical instruction very much like the apostle Paul, saying in essence, be what, by the grace of God, you truly are.

Furthermore, the present tense in this verse indicates clearly that the Father/son relationship still obtained. Though Israel had sinned in the wilderness and broken the covenant, by the grace of Yahweh, the covenant relationship between the Father and the son was not overturned. The rebellious son had been disciplined in the wilderness, but not ultimately rejected.

---

10. סְגֻלָּה only appears eight times in the entire Old Testament (Ex. 19:5; Deut. 7:6; 14:2; 26:18; Mal. 3:17; Ps. 135:4; Ecc. 2:8; 1 Chr. 29:3—the last two are "secular" uses), the first reference being the most significant in Exodus 19:5, where Yahweh declares that Israel shall be His treasured possession.

Deuteronomy 32:5-6, 18-20

The final unambiguous references to Yahweh as father all occur in the Song of Moses (Deut. 32). As we shall see later, the literary context includes allusions to the Fifth Word that assume the Father/son relationship. What distinguishes the Song of Moses from other references to God as Father is that these occur in a song that all Israel was taught to sing, presumably on regular occasions.[11] In other words, the multiple allusions in the song to God's fatherly love and Israel's foolish rebellion were intended to become part of Israel's national consciousness, supplying both comfort and warning, though the emphasis is decidedly on warning of future judgment. Another remarkable feature is that the children of Israel are here referred to as the "sons and daughters" of God (32:19), repeating the perspective of Deuteronomy 14:1, which teaches the people of Israel to think of each individual as God's son or daughter,

---

11. According to Alfred Edersheim, the Song of Moses was a regular part of Israel's Sabbath worship. "At the close of the additional Sabbath sacrifice, when its drink-offering was brought, the Levites sang the 'Song of Moses' in Deuteronomy 32. This 'hymn' was divided into six portions, for as many Sabbaths (vv. 1-6; 7-12; 13-18; 19-28; 29-39; 40-end). Each portion was sung in three sections with threefold blasts of the priests' trumpets, the people worshipping at each pause. If a Sabbath and a 'new moon' fell on the same day, the Sabbath hymn was sung in preference to that for the new moon; if a feast day fell on the Sabbath, the Sabbath sacrifice was offered before that prescribed for the day. At the evening sacrifice on the Sabbath the song of Moses in Exodus 15 was sung." *The Temple: Its Ministry and Services* (Grand Rapids: Christian Classic Ethereal Library, 2000), 96. Online at http://www.ccel.org/ccel/edersheim/temple.html Edersheim is outdated and I am not confident that his material is accurate, but it is certainly the kind of liturgical use of the song that we would expect.

while also regarding the nation as a whole as Yahweh's son.

> They have dealt corruptly with him,
> They are not his sons,
> It is their blemish;
> They are a perverse and crooked generation.
> Do ye thus requite Yahweh,
> O foolish people and unwise?
> Is not he thy father that hath bought thee?
> He hath made thee, and established thee. (32:5–6)

> You neglected the Rock who begot you,
> And forgot the God who gave you birth.[12]
> And Yahweh saw it, and abhorred them,
> Because of the provocation of his sons and his
>   daughters.
> And he said, I will hide my face from them,
> I will see what their end shall be:
> For they are a very perverse generation,
> Sons in whom is no faithfulness. (32:18–20)

The warning that the children of Israel would be disinherited for their idolatry presupposed the Father/son relationship so central to the book of Deuteronomy and the covenant. Yahweh was the Father that bought the

---

12. Though it is possible that both expressions in verse 18 depict Yahweh as Israel's mother, it seems to me perhaps better to see a more complex metaphor. It is likely that Yahweh is seen here both as Israel's father, "the Rock who begot you," and also as Israel's mother, "the God who gave you birth." In verses 10 and 11 of Deuteronomy 32, Yahweh's care for Israel is compared to an eagle's protection of its young, similar to the expression in Exodus 19:4. These also seem to be "mother" images of Yahweh's love. But 32:6 explicitly speaks of Yahweh as father. Therefore, if not in verse 18, at least in the broader context both father and mother metaphors describe Yahweh's love and care.

nation, redeeming it from Egypt because Israel was His firstborn (Ex. 4:22). What the Law required was gratitude and love from the son in response to the love Yahweh had so lavishly poured out on him. But the children of Yahweh were hard-hearted and foolish. They turned away from the true God and worshipped idols. However, near the end of the song, Moses predicted that Yahweh would take vengeance against His enemies (32:43). This is a promise of salvation like that given to Eve in the Garden (Gen. 3:15). It cannot be overemphasized that Moses prophesies that in the end, the Father will bring His prodigal son home.

Conclusion
Though there are only a few direct and clear references to Yahweh's Father/son relationship with Israel, including both individual and national aspects, we have seen that they occur in pregnant historical passages describing the Exodus and Wilderness wandering, in a passage of ethical instruction about righteously bearing the name of Yahweh, and in the song that Moses and Joshua instructed the people to sing from generation to generation. These weighty references establish the importance of the Father/son paradigm. The fact that the first and last references occur in passages that emphasize Israel's disobedience already points to the rebellious son, the other aspect of the paradigm. As we shall see, this basic outline is supported in other parts of Deuteronomy by clear allusions both to the Fifth Word and to the law of the rebellious son.

Chapter Two

The Double Promise of the Fifth Word

The Fifth Word concerns the parent/child relationship, but unlike most of the Ten Words, it includes a promise. In Exodus 20:12, only one promise—the promise of long life—is attached, whereas in Deuteronomy 5:16 the Fifth Word includes a double promise. If children obey their parents, their lives will be long, and it will go well with them in the land. This twofold promise is unique in the Ten Words as they are found in Deuteronomy.

> Honor thy father and thy mother, as Yahweh thy God commanded thee; that thy days may be long, and that it may go well with thee, in the land which Yahweh thy God giveth thee. (Deut. 5:16)

Also in Deuteronomy, Moses places special emphasis on the fact that the Ten Words were the very heart of the Law that God gave to the children of Israel at Mt. Sinai.

> These words Yahweh spake unto all your assembly in the mount out of the midst of the fire, of the cloud, and of the thick darkness, with a great voice: and he added no more. And he wrote them upon two tables of stone, and gave them unto me. (Deut. 5:22; cf. 5:1-5).

Though we know from Israel's history that many of the laws were neglected, including even the festivals, this does not necessarily mean that Israelites were typically ignorant of Moses' instruction. There would certainly have been no excuse for an ancient Israelite not to know at least the Ten Words, for they constituted such a succinct expression of the whole Law that all the people could have and should have been familiar with them, though the actual situation no doubt varied from time to time and place to place. We also know that at times of apostasy the ignorance was appalling. However, during much of Israel's history and in many, if not most, places, one would expect that the Ten Words would have been memorized (cf. Deut. 6:6; 11:18; 17:18-19). At least we can say that in Moses' own day, no godly Israelite should have missed the allusions to the Fifth Word when similar promises appear throughout Deuteronomy, especially given Moses' explicit statements of Yahweh's relationship to Israel as Father.

These allusions occur throughout the book. Before we look at the individual verses, consider just the sheer number of various references. There are four passages in Deuteronomy that include the double promise of long life and blessing in almost exactly the form that it appears in the Fifth Word, "that your days may be prolonged and that it may go well with you" (4:39-40; 5:28-33; 6:1-3; 22:6-7) and two other passages that probably allude to both promises, though in a somewhat different form (6:24; 30:15–16). In addition, there are eight verses in Deuteronomy that only have the promise that the children of Israel will do well (6:18; 8:16; 10:13; 12:25, 28; 19:13; 28:63; 30:5) and seven verses that only have the promise that Israel will live long (4:26; 11:9, 21; 17:20; 25:15; 30:18; 32:47). A few of these verses are warnings that if they do not obey Yahweh's commandments, they will not do well or not live long (4:26; 28:63; 30:18), but the majority of these references are like the Fifth Word itself—expressed so as to encourage obedience by the promise of blessing. Thus, in addition to the six explicit references to God's relationship with Israel as a Father/son relationship (1:31; 8:5; 14:1; 32:5, 19–20), there are about twenty allusions to the promises of the Fifth Word. Together, just in terms of the number of verses, this certainly constitutes a major underlying theme—a poetic refrain that keeps before the reader the proper perspective for seeing the whole.

That there are verses that include both promises of the Fifth Word, especially in a single sentence and using almost identical language—even sometimes using the exact language about the land as well—indicates beyond reasonable doubt that Moses intended for the children of Israel to understand the allusion to the Fifth Word. Through the allusions, Moses' own literary intention is apparent—the children of Israel are to consider Yahweh as their Father and both the nation as His son and individual people as His children.

The full meaning of promise of reward for the faithful child in the home when restated in reference to Yahweh's relationship with Israel must be understood in terms of the blessings promised to the children of Israel in Deuteronomy 28. Even long life—but especially "doing well"—is an ambiguous expression that needs to be filled out. What does it mean to "do well?" The answer is given in the list of specific covenant blessings. In other words, "doing well" in Deuteronomy has a covenantal definition which addresses every aspect of life: agriculture, weather, international political relations, health, child-bearing, and personal happiness.

Since the Father/son relationship is set forth so frequently as the key to blessing and no other theme offers anything like a compelling alternative, it should be apparent that Moses was teaching the Israelites to regard this Father/son relationship as of the very essence of the covenant. If this is true, then the overwhelming emphasis on the Father/son relationship suggests that when Deuteronomy speaks of covenant love, it is primarily, if not exclusively, the love of Father for a son. Israel, the son, is seen as responding to or rejecting the Father's love. By contrast, the marriage metaphor comes to explicit statement in only one verse in Deuteronomy (Deut. 31:16), though it does appear in the other books of the Law (Ex. 34:15–16; Lev. 17:7; 20:5–6; Num. 15:39; 25:1).[1]

---

1. All of these references speak of "playing the harlot" through idolatry. They presuppose the marriage analogy of the covenant, but do not state it directly, whereas the Father/son relationship comes to direct expression. I have not investigated the possibility of other indirect expressions of the Husband/bride metaphor, but there may be some. For example, Deuteronomy frequently uses the word "cling" (דבק), which appears first in Genesis 2:24 speaking of the husband's responsibility to "cling" to his wife. But in Deuteronomy, Moses speaks of Israel clinging to Yahweh. Since Israel would be the "wife" rather than the "husband" in the Deuteronomy metaphor, it seems to me that "cling" better comports with the Father/son metaphor, though Joshua 23:12 may suggest that a "bride" can cling also. It is possible that in references to "cling" the Husband/bride metaphor is mixed with the Father/son metaphor. Jeremiah 3:19–20 places the two relationships side by side, first describing Israel as son, then

Deuteronomy 4:39–40
The first passage with both promises occurs in the concluding statement to a short summary of the Exodus and the giving of the Law at Sinai (4:32–40).

> Know therefore this day, and lay it to thy heart, that Yahweh he is God in heaven above and upon the earth beneath; there is none else. And thou shalt keep his statutes, and his commandments, which I command thee this day, that it may go well with thee, and with thy children after thee, and that thou mayest prolong thy days in the land, which Yahweh thy God giveth thee, for ever. (4:39–40)

The larger paragraph in which 4:39–40 is included (4:32–40) sums up and concludes Moses' words from chapter 1, to give final emphasis on the tremendous grace that has been bestowed upon the children of Israel, just before Moses proceeds to the Ten Words. He reminds them that from the beginning of creation, no other nation has experienced a personal visitation from God in His glory cloud, declaring His covenant. Sinai is unique (4:32–33). Nor has any other nation seen the redemptive power of God as Israel did in the Exodus. Therefore, they should know that Yahweh alone is God (4:34–35). After this declaration of absolute monotheism, Moses continues in the next verses to recount the encounter at Sinai and redemption from Egypt—again in the same reverse chronological order as 4:32–35—Sinai first, Egypt second (4:36–38).

One remarkable feature of this recitation of God's redemptive goodness is the use of the Hebrew word

---

immediately afterwards as wife. Odd as the juxtaposition may seem to us, both relationships find their essence in self-giving love.

יסר, which means "to discipline" (4:36). It is used only four times in the book of Deuteronomy (Deut 4:36; 8:5; 21:18; 22:18), one of which is in the passage about the disobedient son (21:18) and one of which is in a similar context that indicates the frame of reference: parental disciple.

> And thou shalt consider in thy heart, that, as a man chasteneth his son, so Yahweh thy God chasteneth thee. (8:5)

Another important link with the Fifth Word is found in the expression "in the land which Yahweh thy God giveth thee" (4:40). The exact Hebrew expression[2] is used only four times in the entire Old Testament. It appears first in Exodus 20:12 in the original giving of the Fifth Word and in Deuteronomy 5:16 as quoted above. It occurs also in Deuteronomy 25:15, an allusion to the Fifth Word that we will consider later. The present passage, Deuteronomy 4:39–40, is the fourth.

These multiple allusions to the Fifth Word, including depicting God as Israel's disciplining Father in 4:36, make it quite clear that in these verses the image of Yahweh as a loving Father echoes in the background. The allusion to the Fifth Word would be even more clear to the ancient Israelite hearing the text read aloud in Hebrew. It would not be necessary for the word "father" to appear since the double promise and the distinct language about the land from the Fifth Word evoke the Father/son picture of Yahweh's relationship with Israel.

The fact that this first reference to the double promise of the Fifth Word occurs early in Deuteron-

2. עַל הָאֲדָמָה אֲשֶׁר־יְהוָה אֱלֹהֶיךָ נֹתֵן לָךְ:

omy in a crucial passage would have fixed the literary motif in the minds of the ancient readers or hearers. Together with the explicit statement of God's fatherhood in 1:31, this allusion introduces a major theme in Deuteronomy even before the record of the Ten Words. Once the connection had been established clearly between Yahweh's covenant relation to Israel and a father's to his son, other allusions, though not so rich in the use of Fifth Word expressions, would nevertheless have been unmistakable.

Deuteronomy 5:28-33

The next occurrences of the double promise appear in a theologically pregnant context that constitutes perhaps the height of drama in Deuteronomy: the paragraph which concludes the gift of the Ten Words. In Deuteronomy, Moses not only records the Ten Words in a slightly new form, he retells the story of the gift of the commandments in a new form, emphasizing the glory of Yahweh's appearance to the children of Israel and their fear before Him. The allusion to the double promise of the Fifth Word, thus, occurs in one of the most important paragraphs of the entire book. Moreover, in the scope of a mere six verses, the double promise is alluded to twice, adding emphasis to emphasis.

The drama of this paragraph arises from the dialogue between Israel and Yahweh mediated by Moses. The people of Israel express their profound fear of Yahweh's greatness and their desire for Moses to stand between them and Yahweh (5:25-27). To this, Yahweh responds with words only recorded in the book of Deuteronomy (5:28-29)—a passionate expression of fatherly care, one of the most emotionally charged statements ever uttered by Israel's God. And in that very verse (5:29), there is an allusion to the Fifth Word which explicitly cites one of the two promises and echoes the other.

> And Yahweh heard the voice of your words, when ye spake unto me; and Yahweh said unto me, I have heard the voice of the words of this people, which they have spoken unto thee: they have well said all that they have spoken. Oh that there were such a heart in them, that they would fear me, and keep all my commandments always, that it might be well with them, and with their children for ever! (5:28–29)

It is remarkable that Yahweh's response includes this allusion to the Fifth Word, even though only one of the promises comes to exact expression in Yahweh's longing words—"that it may be well with them." However, a careful reading discovers an echo to the other promise, the promise of long life, in the expression "and with their children for ever!" Here, then, we see the compassion and love of the Father expressed in the earnest desire that His children might be blessed.

The reference to fearing Yahweh in this context is suggestive as well, for "fear" is related to the notion of "honor."[3] In Leviticus 19:3, for example, instead of the command to "honor" the parents, at the beginning of the Holiness Code—the central and most important chapter in Leviticus—we have the following.

> And Yahweh spake unto Moses, saying, Speak unto all the congregation of the children of Israel, and say unto them, Ye shall be holy; for I Yahweh your God am holy. Ye shall fear every man his mother,

---

3. Deuteronomy 28:58 expressly puts the two together. "If thou wilt not observe to do all the words of this law that are written in this book, that thou mayest fear this honored and fearful name, Yahweh thy God . . ."

and his father; and ye shall keep my sabbaths: I am
Yahweh your God. (Lev. 19:1-3)

Just as holiness means fearing God, it also means fearing one's father and mother. In Deuteronomy, then, when Moses records Yahweh's fervent yearning for His people—"Oh that they had such a heart in them, that they would fear Me"—the "fear" being referred to should be understood in the light of the Fifth Word.[4] For surely Yahweh is not desiring that the children of Israel, for whom He has already expressed fatherly love, should be terrified of Him, like the nations around Israel would dread and fear Him (Deut. 2:4; 28:10). The children of Israel tended to be afraid of the nations, but Moses repeatedly urged them to trust Yahweh and obey Him (Deut. 1:29-30; 3:22; 7:18, 21; 20:1; 31:6, 8). The fear they should have had for Yahweh was the honor and awe they should have felt for the Great Father who so intensely sought only their blessing.

There is a second allusion to the Fifth Word only a few verses later, in the concluding sentence of the paragraph (5:33). Here Moses paraphrases Yahweh's words and turns them into a command. In so doing, he explicitly alludes to both promises in reverse order as in verse 29. He also paraphrases the reference to the land from the Fifth Word.

> Ye shall walk in all the way which Yahweh your God hath commanded you, that ye may live, and that it may be well with you, and that ye may prolong your days in the land which ye shall possess. (5:33)

---

4. I believe this is true for every reference to fearing Yahweh in Deuteronomy, whatever other nuance may be involved (Deut. 4:10; 5:29; 6:2, 13, 24; 8:6; 10:12, 20; 13:4; 14:23; 17:19; 28:58; 31:12-13).

It is hard to exaggerate the significance of this double allusion to the promises of the Fifth Word occurring in the climactic paragraph of the chapter on the Ten Words. Add to this that the first of the allusions comes in a quotation of Yahweh which can only be described as an expression of tender and passionate fatherly care.

The very essence of the covenant—the Ten Words—is presented to us in Deuteronomy in the language of the Father/son relationship. Moses adds his own emphasis on this at the most appropriate place in the book, so that we would not miss his meaning. The "law" of the covenant is the word of the Father. The exposition of the Ten Words which follows (6–26), having been prefaced by unquestionable allusions to the Fifth Word, is securely locked in this family framework. By Deuteronomy 5, not only has the Father/son paradigm already been set before us repeatedly, it has come to expression in one of the most theologically profound and dramatically intense contexts in the entire book. Even if the allusion to the Fifth Word did not occur in all the rest of the book, this climactic paragraph in chapter 5 alone would establish the paradigm as the fundamental perspective for understanding God's relationship to Israel.

Deuteronomy 6:1–3

Now emphasis is added to emphasis. The profound statement on the Father/son relationship at the end of chapter 5 finds immediate restatement in the first words of chapter 6. In chapter 5, the double allusion to the Fifth Word came at the end of the giving of the Ten Words. In the immediately following verses at the beginning of chapter 6, the allusion to the Fifth Word appears in a paragraph that introduces the exposition of the Law in chapters 6–26 (6:1–3).[5] Once again, then, the allusion to the Fifth Word comes at a crucial literary junction, adding weight to its meaning. Considering the closeness of the previous allusions, the emphasis on the Father/son relationship in this section of Deuteronomy stands out remarkably. Close attention to the words of 6:1–3 suggests the reason for this emphasis.

> Now this is the commandment, the statutes, and the ordinances, which Yahweh your God commanded me to teach you, that ye might do them in the land whither ye go over to possess it; that thou mightest fear Yahweh thy God, to keep all his statutes and his commandments, which I command thee, thou, and thy son, and thy son's son, all the days of thy life; and that thy days may be prolonged.
> Hear therefore, O Israel, and observe to do it; that it may be well with thee, and that ye may increase mightily, as Yahweh, the God of thy fathers, hath promised unto thee, in a land flowing with milk and honey. (6:1–3)

Introducing the chapters in Deuteronomy that contain the detailed stipulations of the covenant is a short paragraph with a double call for the children of Israel to obey the covenant. The first call is not stated as an imperative, but it is clear that Moses is not here simply informing us that God commanded him to teach Israel so that they would fear Yahweh and keep His commandments in order to be blessed. The second call is stated straightforwardly as a call to obedience to

---

5. The literary break with the previous context at 6:1 is clear, and 6:4 obviously introduces the next section, so 6:1–3 functions as an introductory paragraph at least for the entire section continuing to the end of chapter 12, and most likely for the entire third aspect of the covenant, extending to chapter 26:19.

the covenant. Note that each call is followed by a promise from the Fifth Word, the first call by the first promise and the second call by the second promise. Note also that there is also a double reference to the land (vss. 1, 3) and another reference to fearing Yahweh. In 6:1-3, Moses is alluding to the immediately preceding words, as well as to the Fifth Word.

In the phrase "this is the commandment," the word "commandment" (הַמִּצְוָה) is singular, and is used to refer to the whole Law, as it does in every instance in Deuteronomy when the singular noun occurs with the definite article.[6] The whole covenant of Moses is the subject of concern in the double call. The heading for the extended application of the Ten Words, thus, instructs the children of Israel to think of Yahweh as their heavenly Father and to fear Him accordingly, assured that He delights to bless them in the land with long life and well-being.

This serves the same literary purpose as the double allusion to the Fifth Word in the concluding paragraph of chapter 5. At the beginning of the exposition of the Law, Moses places the whole Law, all of its statues and ordinances, in the context of the Father/son relationship between Yahweh and the children of Israel, defining the nature of the covenant from the beginning.

---

6. There are thirteen occasions of the singular noun used with the definite article (Deut. 5:31; 6:1, 25; 7:11; 8:1; 11:8, 22; 15:5; 17:20; 19:9; 27:1; 30:11; 31:5). In three of these, the phrase occurs with "the statues and the judgments" (הַחֻקִּים וְהַמִּשְׁפָּטִים), indicating that the singular command is a statement for all that is included in the detailed commandments (Deut. 5:31; 6:1; 7:11). There are nine occurrences of the expression "all this command" (כָּל־הַמִּצְוָה) (Deut. 5:31; 6:25; 8:1; 11:8, 22; 15:5; 19:9; 27:1; 31:5), again pointing to the singular noun "command" as a synonym with "law."

Deuteronomy 22:6-7

The final indisputable example of referring to both of the promises of the Fifth Word is found in the law in Deuteronomy 22:6-7.

> If a bird's nest chance to be before thee in the way, in any tree or on the ground, with young ones or eggs, and the dam sitting upon the young, or upon the eggs, thou shalt not take the dam with the young: thou shalt surely let the dam go, but the young thou mayest take unto thyself; that it may be well with thee, and that thou mayest prolong thy days. (22:6-7)

This law is near the end of the section of Deuteronomy that expounds the implications of the Sixth Word (19:1–22:8). The relationship between individual laws and the Sixth Word are not always apparent, but since there is sufficient evidence for viewing chapters 6–26 as structured in terms of the Ten Words,[7] it seems legitimate to consider the less obvious cases in terms of the larger paradigm. The commandment which forbids us to kill is somehow relevant for the way that we treat birds, and by extension, animals in general. The specific case of the most helpless and defenseless defines the general view—typical of the way Israel's God cares for the weak.

More significant for this essay, however, is that the law concerns mother and child. To take the parent and the child together seems to be regarded as cruel or disrespectful of life. But underlying this is the Fifth Word. Since the children of Israel have been taught to

---

7. See James B. Jordan, *Covenant Sequence in Leviticus and Deuteronomy* (Tyler, TX: Institute for Christian Economics, 1989), 57-69.

see themselves as God's children and been promised special blessings for obedience, there naturally arises a special respect for the parent/child relationship even among animals, especially among the weakest and most insignificant. The helplessness of the bird is an important aspect of the law so that this law combines kindness to the helpless with respect for the parent/child relationship. Of all the many detailed commandments that could be emphasized by including the double promise, God led Moses to apply it here. Given Israel's agricultural society, there must have been many occasions to recall this law and to be encouraged to obey, so that Yahweh the Father would bless them with the blessings of the Fifth Word: "that it may be well with thee, and that thou mayest prolong thy days."

Deuteronomy 6:24 and 30:15–16

In addition to the very clear allusions above, there also seem to be allusions to the double promise in Deuteronomy 6:24 and 30:15–16. The language is not exact, but it is close. In both passages the similar language is associated with other expressions that allude to the Fifth Word.

> And Yahweh commanded us to do all these statutes, to fear Yahweh our God, for our good always, that he might preserve us alive, as at this day. (6:24)

> See, I have set before thee this day life and good, and death and evil; in that I command thee this day to love Yahweh thy God, to walk in his ways, and to keep his commandments and his statutes and his ordinances, that thou mayest live and multiply, and that Yahweh thy God may bless thee in the land whither thou goest in to possess it. (30:15–16)

In 6:24, the Hebrew translated "for our good always" is quite close to the Hebrew in the Fifth Word,[8] and the expression "preserve us alive" used in association with the "for our good" and the promise of the land (6:23) almost certainly is intended to provoke recollection of the promises of the Fifth Word.

In 30:15–16, though the expression "long life" does not appear, Moses says he sets "life" before them and urges them to keep God's commandments so that they may "live and multiply." This corresponds to the first of the two promises. The other promise is given in the expression "that it may go well with you." In 30:15, the same Hebrew word appears when Moses says, "I have set before thee . . . good . . ." In verse 16, the promise of blessing corresponds to the promise of well-being in the Fifth Word. The expression "walk in His ways" is also associated with the Father/son metaphor, as Deuteronomy 8:5–6 makes clear.

Conclusion

We have seen that allusions to the double promise of the Fifth Word are quite unambiguous. They occur in some of the most crucial verses in the book of Deuteronomy, reinforcing the emphasis of the repeated explicit references to Yahweh as Israel's Father. Overall, they contribute with other allusions and direct statements to define the heart of Yahweh's covenant with Israel. Moses' primary intention in alluding to the promises of the Fifth Word is to motivate the children of Israel to obey Yahweh. The nature of the Father/son relationship is set forth in terms of the Father's tender care, so that the children of Israel know that the Fa-

---

8. In 6:24 the Hebrew is לְטוֹב לָנוּ and in 5:16 the Hebrew is לְךָ יִיטַב. The Fifth Word is stated in the verbal form, whereas in 6:24 the form is adjectival. The allusion is nonetheless clear.

ther desires to and delights in blessing His people, just like earthly fathers who know how to give good gifts to their children. The repeated promises of long life and well-being serve as shorthand for the whole spectrum of covenant blessings, setting before the people a vision of cultural, political, and personal peace and prosperity (Deut. 28:1–14).

Chapter Three

A Single Promise From the Fifth Word

As we have seen, important passages in Deuteronomy specifically expressing Yahweh's fatherhood over the children of Israel combine with clear allusions to both promises of the Fifth Word to define the paradigm for the covenant relationship between Yahweh and Israel. But there are many more allusions to the Fifth Word in the form of partial quotations of the language of one or the other of the two promises. Again, these are sufficiently unambiguous as to constitute a recurring sub-theme, a refrain that keeps the Father/son relationship present to the consciousness of the reader or hearer of Deuteronomy.

The Promise of Prolonged Days

There are seven allusions to the first of the promises attached to the Fifth Word, the promise of long life, "that your days may be prolonged" (Deut. 5:16; Ex. 20:12). Two of these are included in prophetic warnings that Israel will not prolong her days (4:26; 30:18). One of them is specifically applied to the king

(17:20). The allusions are spread out throughout the book of Deuteronomy, beginning in chapter four.

Deuteronomy 4:26

Although this occurs before the first allusion to both promises and before the statement of the Fifth Word in Deuteronomy, the first allusion to the first promise is in a prophetic warning context, one which presupposes the whole Father/son paradigm introduced in chapter 1, including an echo to the law of the rebellious son. The prophetic warning against apostasy, though not specifically using language related to the rebellious son, reminds us that the son would transgress the covenant and face judgment.

> When thou shalt beget children, and children's children, and ye shall have been long in the land, and shall corrupt yourselves, and make a graven image in the form of anything, and shall do that which is evil in the sight of Yahweh thy God, to provoke him to anger; I call heaven and earth to witness against you this day, that ye shall soon utterly perish from off the land whereunto ye go over the Jordan to possess it; ye shall not prolong your days upon it, but shall utterly be destroyed. (Deut. 4:25–26)

The phrase "ye shall not prolong your days" (יָמִים לֹא־תַאֲרִיכֻן) differs only slightly from the positive form of the promise in the commandment in which "days" is the subject, "your days shall be prolonged" (יַאֲרִכֻן יָמֶיךָ). In specifically denying that Israel would inherit the blessing of the obedient child because of committing evil that provokes Yahweh to anger, Moses links Israel with the son so evil his own parents have to call for him to be punished.

Deuteronomy 11:8-9

The section of the Law applying the First Word began with allusions to the Fifth Word (6:1-3) and now it ends with allusions to the Fifth Word. Within the application of the First Word (6-11), Moses follows the five-aspect covenant outline.[1] Deuteronomy 11:8-9 expresses the third aspect of the covenant—ethical instruction. Moses' intention here is to encourage. He urges Israel to obey the whole Law, all of the instruction Yahweh gave to Israel, in order that they might become strong. The allusion to the Abrahamic covenant—"the land which Yahweh sware unto your fathers to give them"—reminds them that Yahweh keeps His covenant. Moses further encourages them by describing the land as "flowing with milk and honey." The exhortation expresses the earnest concern of a father who seeks his son's well being.

> Therefore shall ye keep all the commandment which I command thee this day, that ye may be strong, and go in and possess the land, whither ye go

---

1. James Jordan outlines Deuteronomy 6-11 in terms of the five aspects of the covenant, repeated twice. *Covenant Sequence*, 37.

    A. The Covenant Made at Sinai:
        1. The God of Israel, 6:1-19
        2. Initial Deliverance from Egypt, 6:20-25
        3. Commandment, 7:1-11
        4. Sanctions, 7:12-16
        5. Continuity, 7:17-26

    B. The Covenant Renewed after Being Broken:
        1. The God of Israel and His sovereign choice, 8:1-9:6
        2. Breakdown and Renewal, 9:7-10:11
        3. Commandment, 10:12-11:12
        4. Sanction, 11:13-17
        5. Continuity, 11:18-32

over to possess it; and that ye may prolong your days in the land, which Yahweh sware unto your fathers to give unto them and to their seed, a land flowing with milk and honey. (Deut. 11:8–9)

Deuteronomy 11:20–21

This same spirit of earnest fatherly persuasion continues through the end of the chapter—or rather pervades the whole book of Deuteronomy. Just as Moses began the section on the application of the First Word by calling for parents to teach their children diligently (6:1–3), he also brings the instruction on the First Word to a close by repeating the same instruction, also repeating the allusion to the Fifth Word. To make clear the relationship with chapter 6:4–9, I quote a passage that includes more than the allusion to the promise, which comes near the end and is stated with extra emphasis on this occasion, "as the days of heaven above the earth." Note also the allusion to the Abrahamic covenant.[2]

> Therefore shall ye lay up these my words in your heart and in your soul; and ye shall bind them for a sign upon your hand, and they shall be for frontlets between your eyes. And ye shall teach them your children, talking of them, when thou sittest in thy house, and when thou walkest by the way, and when thou liest down, and when thou risest up. And thou shalt write them upon the door-posts of thy house, and upon thy gates; that your days may be multiplied, and the days of your children, in the land which Yahweh sware unto your fathers to give

---

2. Deuteronomy has eleven allusions to the Abrahamic covenant using the Hebrew expression "which Yahweh sware" (יְהוָה אֲשֶׁר נִשְׁבַּע—1:8; 2:14; 6:18; 8:1; 9:5; 11:9, 21; 26:3; 28:11; 30:20; 31:7).

them, as the days of the heavens above the earth.
(Deut. 11:18–21)

Deuteronomy 17:20

Deuteronomy 17:20 occurs in the law for the future king. Even without this law, previous revelation plainly revealed Yahweh's will that the people of Israel eventually have a monarchy, for the promised Messiah was to be a King and the Abrahamic promise included the promise that kings would come from Abraham (Gen. 17:6, 16; 35:11). What the law in Deuteronomy added was unambiguous Biblical restrictions on the authority of the king, making the ancient Israelite understanding of kingship quite different from that of the surrounding nations of the day. Israel's was to be a constitutional monarchy.

To summarize the negative instruction, the king was forbidden to amass horses, wives, and gold (Deut. 17:16–17). Horses were the most powerful weapon for aggressive warfare in the ancient world, just like walls were the essence of self-defense in the age before cannons could easily topple them. Forbidding the king to buy horses from Egypt was equivalent to forbidding the king from building an aggressive army. Requiring monogamy of the king meant that he set the example for the nation in marriage. Commanding the king not to acquire large amounts of gold amounts to a restriction on his rights to tax the people.[3]

---

3. Though the expression "multiply for himself gold" is not exact, it seems most reasonable to understand it as referring to excessive taxation. But there is no specification in this text or anywhere else in the Law of Moses to indicate exactly what it would mean for the king to "over tax" the people. Perhaps the fact that Yahweh demanded one tenth provided a sort of rule for the king. He should not demand more than Yahweh.

In addition to the negative laws limiting the king's authority, there was a positive law as well.

> And it shall be, when he sitteth upon the throne of his kingdom, that he shall write him a copy of this law in a book, out of that which is before the priests the Levites: and it shall be with him, and he shall read therein all the days of his life; that he may learn to fear Yahweh his God, to keep all the words of this law and these statutes, to do them; that his heart be not lifted up above his brethren, and that he turn not aside from the commandment, to the right hand, or to the left: to the end that he may prolong his days in his kingdom, he and his children, in the midst of Israel. (Deut. 17:18–20)

The law presupposes that the king himself will learn to read and write, not necessarily normal in the ancient world. It furthermore requires that his own copy of the Law be written by his own hand. This means that he would have to learn scribal technique, at least to a degree, for the ancient scribes had strict rules to prevent the entrance of errors into the text. Reading the Law daily no doubt meant reading it out loud. Though it is not specifically so stated, the presence of scribes both at the writing and the reading of the Law is probably assumed.

The purpose of the positive command is the most striking aspect of this teaching. The daily reading out of the Law which had been written by the king's own hand was intended to prevent the king from becoming proud, regarding himself as better than his brethren, and also to protect him from wandering away from the right path. The ultimate end was that the king might prolong his days in his kingdom, as Yahweh's faithful son. Israel's monarch was Yahweh. Deuteronomy was the constitution. The human monarch was a man under authority, ruling for Yahweh to bless the people of Israel.

By having one Law for the king and the people and by indicating clearly that the king himself was under the authority of Yahweh's Law just as the people, the Torah set a rule that was to protect the freedom and dignity of the people of Israel. The people were not the king's slaves, but his brothers. In contrast to Pharaoh, the supposed half-god, half-man king of Egypt, Israel's king was not different from his people in nature. Thus, the institution of the monarchy in ancient Israel defined the people of Yahweh distinctly from the other nations in order to bring blessing on Israel and to give them a testimony to the nations around them (Deut. 4:6–8).

Finally, it is important to note that the king is understood here to embody the nation in a manner of speaking. Throughout Deuteronomy, the promises of the Fifth Word are applied to the nation as a whole, but in Deuteronomy 17:20, the promise of long life belongs to the king and his godly descendants. This could be seen as an application of the promise to an individual, and certainly there is a general implication that individuals who keep the covenant enjoy the promises of the Fifth Word because they honor their heavenly Father. But that is not likely to be the point of Deuteronomy 17:20. Rather, as the text says, the king was in "the midst of Israel," and he was not to have "heart lifted up above his brothers." He was to be the true Israelite, who led the nation by his example of humbly following God's word. The promise, therefore, has more than simply an individualistic meaning. As the nation's representative, the king's filial love and obedience to Yahweh would bring blessing on the whole people.

Deuteronomy 25:15

The present passage fits into Moses' application of the Tenth Word, "Thou shalt not covet." By forbidding the use of an unjust weight, the command aims at premeditated covetousness, not just the act of stealing itself.

> Thou shalt not have in thy bag diverse weights, a great and a small. Thou shalt not have in thy house diverse measures, a great and a small. A perfect and just weight shalt thou have; a perfect and just measure shalt thou have: that thy days may be long in the land which Yahweh thy God giveth thee. For all that do such things, even all that do unrighteously, are an abomination unto Yahweh thy God. (Deut. 25:13–16)

A man who plans ahead to cheat his customers—in ancient Israel most of whom would be friends and neighbors—by having differing weights and measures is the worst kind of thief, pretending to serve his customers and offer them goods they need while actually deceiving them. Since the amount stolen is small, the dishonest businessman may not be conscious of it, but he has made stealing his profession. The pettiness of it only aggravates the nature of the crime. A man must be deeply covetous to lust for such small gain.

In addition, Moses statement that the pilferer's ways are an abomination is significant. In Deuteronomy, the word "תּוֹעֵבָה" (abomination) is used seventeen times, most commonly in reference to idolatry (Deut. 7:25–26; 12:31; 13:14; 14:3; 17:1, 4; 18:9, 12; 20:18; 22:5; 23:18; 24:4; 25:16; 27:15; 32:16). Since Moses is expounding the Tenth Word in his context, it seems legitimate to assume that he presupposes exactly the connection that the apostle Paul makes: covetousness is idolatry (Col. 3:5). The idolater will not enjoy the blessing of long life from Father Yahweh, but will be brought under the judgments of the covenant.

Deuteronomy 30:18, 20

The last paragraph of the fourth major division of the book of Deuteronomy is the concluding exhortation in Moses' exposition of the blessings and curses of the covenant. The whole paragraph is worth quoting because the promises of life are interconnected and part of an exhortation to choose the way of blessing.

> See, I have set before thee this day life and good, and death and evil; in that I command thee this day to love Yahweh thy God, to walk in his ways, and to keep his commandments and his statutes and his ordinances, that thou mayest live and multiply, and that Yahweh thy God may bless thee in the land whither thou goest in to possess it. But if thy heart turn away, and thou wilt not hear, but shalt be drawn away, and worship other gods, and serve them; I denounce unto you this day, that ye shall surely perish; ye shall not prolong your days in the land, whither thou passest over the Jordan to go in to possess it. I call heaven and earth to witness against you this day, that I have set before thee life and death, the blessing and the curse: therefore choose life, that thou mayest live, thou and thy seed; to love Yahweh thy God, to obey his voice, and to cleave unto him; for he is thy life, and the length of thy days; that thou mayest dwell in the land which Yahweh sware unto thy fathers, to Abraham, to Isaac, and to Jacob, to give them. (Deut. 30:15–20)

Moses' very first words in this paragraph should probably be seen as an allusion to the promises of the Fifth Word, as I argued in the previous chapter, even though the language is not exactly borrowed from it.

Thus, the paragraph begins by addressing the children of Israel as Yahweh's children. After earnestly urging the Israelites to love Yahweh and walk in His ways, Moses warns them that if they turn away and worship other gods, they will lose the blessing of the Fifth Word: "ye shall not prolong your days in the land" (30:18).

Moses concludes by repeating the exhortation to love Yahweh, to obey Him, and to cleave to Him. The allusion to the promise of the Fifth Word in verse 20 does not borrow the exact language of the promise itself, but "length of days" and "in the land" are such close parallels to the language of the Fifth Word that the allusion seems indubitable. Add to this the particular emphasis on life in this last section of the paragraph.

> I have set before thee life . . . therefore choose life, that thou mayest live . . . for he is thy life and the length of thy days . . .

What is especially outstanding in these final words is that Moses expresses so clearly the very heart of the covenant: Yahweh is thy life and length of days! The essence of the covenant and the focus of all covenantal exhortation is Yahweh Himself. To love Him, obey Him, cling to Him, and walk in His ways is to choose Him, and resultantly to choose life and blessing. This is not the language of a contract or economic calculation. Yahweh the Father, through the fatherly figure of Moses, entreats His beloved children to respond to His love with love.

Deuteronomy 32:47

As we saw in chapter 1, the Song of Moses contains multiple explicit references to Yahweh's fatherhood. It is not surprising, then, that his final words of exhortation revisit the theme by alluding to the promise of life.

> And Moses made an end of speaking all these words to all Israel. And he said unto them, Set your heart unto all the words which I testify unto you this day, which ye shall command your children to observe to do, even all the words of this law. For it is no vain word for you.[4] Indeed it is your life. And by this word ye shall prolong your days in the land, whither ye go over the Jordan to possess it. (Deut. 32:45–47)

In three sentences, Moses has used the word דָּבָר (word) five times, including both singular and plural occurrences. The repetition here accords with the allusion in verse 46 in the words "Set your heart unto all the words," which points back to Deuteronomy 11:18.

> Therefore shall ye lay up these my words in your heart and in your soul; and ye shall bind them for a sign upon your hand, and they shall be for frontlets between your eyes.

The closeness of the language may not be apparent to the English reader, but the same verb שִׂים is used in

---

4. Translations of Deuteronomy 32:47 vary because the Hebrew דָּבָר means both "word" and "thing" or "matter." The ASV and the KJV translate both occurrences as "thing" and the NRSV similarly translates as "matter." The NASB and the ESV translate both as "word." The NKJV translates the first occurrence as "thing" and the second as "word." Reading verse 47 in the context of the concluding exhortation and its profound emphasis on the words Moses is speaking persuades me that "word" is the correct translation here. Though the singular דָּבָר often means "thing" or "matter," it may also refer to the whole Law or to a word from Yahweh (cf. Deut 4:2; 5:5; 9:5; 17:11; 18:20–22; 30:14). I have modified the ASV above.

both verses, though the English translation varies ("set," or "lay up"), and both verses are an exhortation to place Yahweh's words in relation to the heart.[5] Furthermore, Deuteronomy 11:18, though using different language, clearly alludes back to Deuteronomy 6:4–9, the paragraph which begins Moses' treatment of the First Word. Deuteronomy 32:45–47, therefore, alludes to the repeated exhortation to have the word of Yahweh inscribed in one's heart and adds that the word of Yahweh, like Yahweh Himself, "is your life." The promise of long life here brings to mind the oneness between Yahweh and His word and the nature of the covenant as a Father/son relationship.

The Promise of Well-Being

The promise of well-being for children who obey their parents is distinctive of Deuteronomy's form of the Fifth Word; in Exodus, the only promise with the Fifth Word is the promise of long life. A modern reader could view the two promises as well-defined and different from one another. It is one thing to live long; it is something else to live well, whether life is short or long. But it is certain that Moses does not intend for us to view the promises this way. Each entails the other, for the promises are promises of blessing. No one in Moses' day, or ours, would regard it as a blessing to have a long life that was not good, nor to have a good life that was cut short.

However, the expression "that it may go well with you in the land" may be capable of a greater variety of synonymous expressions than the promise of long life. The Hebrew verb יטב is related to the noun טוב which is translated in various ways: goodness, prosperity,

---

5. In 11:18, the words are to be "set in" the heart; in 32:46, the heart is to be "set to" the words.

happiness, and so forth.⁶ Synonymous Hebrew words might also be alluding to the Fifth Word, especially when used as a promise for obedience, connected to the expression "in the land," or associated with the promise of life. For this study, I will be restricting myself to the clearest allusions to the Fifth Word, but I believe there are others.

Perhaps Moses, in Deuteronomy, added the promise of well-being to the Exodus promise of long life because "well-being" carries with it broader connotations. But there may also be a significant literary reason. Among the relatively few uses of the expression טוֹב לְ (good to)—it appears only nine times in the Pentateuch, six of which are in Deuteronomy (Deut. 5:33; 6:24; 10:13; 15:16; 19:13; 23:16)—it is no doubt significant that its first three occurrences are on the lips of the children of Israel where they are speaking about it being better for them not in the Promised Land, but in Egypt.

> For it were better for us (טוֹב לָנוּ) to serve the Egyptians (Exo. 14:12)
>
> ... for it was well with us (טוֹב לָנוּ) in Egypt (Num. 11:18)⁷
>
> ... were it not better for us (טוֹב לָנוּ) to return into Egypt? (Num. 14:3).

---

6. See the relevant articles in HALOT and TWOT.

7. Numbers 11:18 seems to be a verbal form, while Exodus 14:12 and Numbers 14:3 are adjectival, but the difference in grammatical form is not important in this case. See Deuteronomy 5:33, a clear allusion to the Fifth Word, which uses the verbal form, and Deuteronomy 6:24, another clear allusion, which uses the adjectival form.

It seems likely that by adding the second promise of well-being in Deuteronomy 5:16, Moses is alluding to the children of Israel's repeated contention that Egypt is better than the Promised Land. In particular, Numbers 14:3 stands out, for this is the context of the decisive act of apostasy. The children of Israel cried out that the land of Egypt was better than the Promised Land and they determined to appoint a leader to take them back. It was this decision that resulted in the thirty-eight years of wandering in the wilderness, waiting for the stiff-necked first generation to die out, while Yahweh trained the next generation in obedience.

It is as if the promise of well-being says, "Contrary to what your rebellious fathers thought, it will be well with you in the land Yahweh gives." Thus, the promise of well-being in the land may include the irony of contrasting a promise of blessing to Israel's hard-hearted preference for Egypt. If this is correct, we may also detect an echo of the theme of the rebellious son.

Deuteronomy 6:18

In the entire Old Testament there are only eight occurrences of the exact Hebrew expression used in the promise of well-being in the Fifth Word לְמַעַן יִיטַב ל, "in order that it may go well with" (Gen. 12:13; Deut. 5:16, 29; 6:18; 12:25, 28; 22:7; Jer. 7:23). The passage in Jeremiah alludes to Deuteronomy and the Fifth Word. Of the five occurrences in Deuteronomy apart from the Fifth Word, two of them allude to both of the promises (5:29; 22:7). That the other three (6:18; 12:25, 28) allude to the Fifth Word can hardly be doubted.

In the context of 6:18, Moses is warning the Israelites not to tempt Yahweh, as they did at Massah, but rather to keep His commandments, so that it will go well with them.

> Ye shall not tempt Yahweh your God, as ye tempted him in Massah. Ye shall diligently keep the commandments of Yahweh your God, and his testimonies, and his statutes, which he hath commanded thee. And thou shalt do that which is right and good in the sight of Yahweh; that it may be well with thee, and that thou mayest go in and possess the good land which Yahweh sware unto thy fathers, to thrust out all thine enemies from before thee, as Yahweh hath spoken. (Deut. 6:16–19)

Possessing the land which Yahweh swore to the fathers was still future for the original audience to whom Moses was preaching the words of Deuteronomy, so possession of the land is here expressed as a blessing given as a result of doing what is right and good in the eyes of Yahweh. In other words, the blessing of well-being for Yahweh's obedient sons enables the conquest. Long life in the land was promised to the Israelites on the presupposition of the future conquest, but the promise of well-being both precedes and succeeds the conquest (6:18 cf. 5:16).

Deuteronomy 8:16

This passage also refers to the time before Israel is in the land and enjoying its blessings. Yahweh's fatherhood over the nation is explicitly referred to in 8:5 where Moses explains that His testing and humbling Israel in the wilderness was His fatherly discipline. In 8:16, Moses is repeating the point in different words, this time pointing to Yahweh's Fatherly love by an allusion to the promise of the Fifth Word. But instead of being a reminder of His care in the wilderness, the paragraph that begins with verse 11 is a warning that begins with "Beware lest thou forget Yahweh thy God." In the ASV, the same sentence continues from verse 11 to verse 17. Verse 16 is the part of the warning in which the children of Israel are reminded of Yahweh's care.

> . . . who fed thee in the wilderness with manna, which thy fathers knew not; that he might humble thee, and that he might prove thee, to do thee good at thy latter end. (Deut. 8:16)

Father Yahweh, even when He is disciplining His children and leading them through a hard way, does so because of His love and His desire to do them good in the end. Yahweh's Fatherly love precedes His son's obedience and also follows it. Even the generation which was punished with death because of its rebellion—a generation which did not deserve to be blessed—enjoyed Yahweh's covenant faithfulness and kindness. He was leading them in the wilderness to do them good.

Deuteronomy 10:13

The context for Deuteronomy 10:13 is Moses' application of the First Word (Deut. 6–11). As we saw previously,[8] the whole section is structured in terms of the five aspects of the covenant, the same structure as the whole book of Deuteronomy. Deuteronomy 10:13 occurs near the beginning of the rather long application of the third aspect of the covenant, ethical instruction (10:12–11:12). The section begins with a question that summarizes the essence of the Law and Yahweh's purpose in giving it.

> And now, Israel, what doth Yahweh thy God require of thee, but to fear Yahweh thy God, to walk in all

---

8. See chapter 2, footnote 6.

his ways, and to love him, and to serve Yahweh thy God with all thy heart and with all thy soul, to keep the commandments of Yahweh, and his statutes, which I command thee this day for thy good? (Deut. 10:12–13)

As a loving Father, Yahweh gave Israel commandments and statutes to guide them in the way of blessing. What He requires is that the children of Israel respond to His love with love. Again the nature of the covenant as a loving Father/son relationship is prominent. Moses himself appeals to Israel repeatedly to win their hearts to motivate them to keep the Law. As a father to the people, it is his earnest desire that they inherit the good their heavenly Father intends for them.

A king may be a tyrant and command people arbitrarily for what he conceives to be his own good, with no thought for the good of the people. But a loving father commands his children for their good; though, of course, earthly fathers may mistake what is actually for the good of their children. Yahweh, the heavenly Father, knows what is good for Israel and so gives His beloved children commandments for their well-being. The whole Law must be read and understood from this perspective.

Deuteronomy 12:25

In Deuteronomy 12:25, the promise of well-being is associated with one of the most important ceremonial prohibitions in the Law.

> Only be sure that thou eat not the blood: for the blood is the life; and thou shalt not eat the life with the flesh. Thou shalt not eat it; thou shalt pour it out upon the earth as water. Thou shalt not eat it; that it may go well with thee, and with thy children

after thee, when thou shalt do that which is right in the eyes of Yahweh. (Deut. 12:23-25)

In Deuteronomy, this prohibition is part of the exposition of the Second Word in Deuteronomy 12-13. Eating the blood is associated with idolatry probably in the sense that the idolator seeks to get life directly from the life of the slain animal or, as in many ancient societies, from the life of slain humans, whether enemies killed in battle or people offered as sacrifice. In the Law, life comes through the death of the sacrificial substitute because life comes from God who forgives us our sins and grants us His grace and favor.

What is important to note here is the ultimate positive purpose for the Law. Contrary to the slander of Satan in the Garden, Yahweh does not prohibit in order to cheat Israel from the enjoyment of higher life, but to bless them and give them the blessings of the covenant, as He promised them.

Deuteronomy 12:28
Only a few verses after Deuteronomy 12:25, there is another allusion to the Fifth Word's promise of well-being.

> Observe and hear all these words which I command thee, that it may go well with thee, and with thy children after thee for ever, when thou doest that which is good and right in the eyes of Yahweh thy God. (Deut. 12:28)

In the context of Deuteronomy 12, verse 28 is part of the last paragraph that sums up Israel's duty to follow the commandments of Yahweh and to avoid the idolatry of the Canaanites. Verse 28 alludes back to verse 1 of chapter 12, bringing it to a conclusion. The paragraph that begins with verse 28 is a chiasmus that emphasizes the teaching of the whole of chapter 12.

> A. Observe and hear all these words which I command thee, that it may go well with thee, and with thy children after thee for ever, when thou doest that which is good and right in the eyes of Yahweh thy God. (28)
> B. When Yahweh thy God shall cut off the nations from before thee, whither thou goest in to dispossess them, and thou dispossessest them, and dwellest in their land; take heed to thyself that thou be not ensnared to follow them, after that they are destroyed from before thee; and that thou inquire not after their gods, saying, How do these nations serve their gods? even so will I do likewise. (29-30)
> B′ Thou shalt not do so unto Yahweh thy God: for every abomination to Yahweh, which he hateth, have they done unto their gods; for even their sons and their daughters do they burn in the fire to their gods. (31)
> A′ What thing soever I command you, that shall ye observe to do: thou shalt not add thereto, nor diminish from it. (32)

Deuteronomy 12 as a whole is a strong warning not to follow the ways of the nations in the Promised Land, but it also includes a warning for the children of Israel not to continue in their present ways (12:8) couched in language that appears later in the book of Judges, clearly suggesting a lax attitude toward Yahweh Himself and His Law.

> Ye shall not do after all the things that we do here this day, every man whatsoever is right in his own eyes. (12:8; cf. Judg 17:6; 21:25)

The children of Israel can only maintain true worship by following in the way of Yahweh's commands. Then they will be blessed. It will go well with them as obedient children who follow Yahweh Himself and not the ways of the nations, who even sacrifice their own children in fire to the gods. Unless Israel does what is right in the eyes of Yahweh, it will not go well with them.

Deuteronomy 19:13

This verse occurs in the exposition of the Sixth Word. The Sixth Word parallels the First Word since the Ten Words repeat the five aspects of the covenant twice, though the relationships between the commandments are more complex than a simple parallel to the five aspects of the covenant. Nevertheless, murdering one made in God's image and likeness is a form of rejecting God as Lord and dishonoring Him.

The expression "innocent blood" (דָּם נָקִי)[9] occurs repeatedly in Deuteronomy (Deut. 19:10, 13; 21:8-9; 27:25), as in the rest of the Old Testament (Josh. 2:19; 1 Sam. 19:5; 2 Sam. 3:28; 2 Kings 21:16; 24:4; Isa. 59:7; Jer. 2:34; 7:6; 19:4; 22:3, 17; 26:15; Joel 3:19; Jonah 1:14; Psa. 94:21; 106:38; Prov. 1:11; 6:17). Though there is no mention of Cain and Abel by name, in these references, there is an unmistakable echo of the story of Cain in 19:11-13.[10] However, even if there had been no link to actual expressions or words used in Genesis 4, the association of ideas is too strong to deny an allusion to the story of the first murder. When innocent

---

9. Sometimes with, sometimes without the article attaching to one or the other word.

10. The verb for "rise up" (קוּם) is quite common in the Old Testament, but it is not commonly used with אל in the sense of "rise up against." Genesis 4:8—"Cain rose up against Abel his brother, and slew him"—is the first use of this expression and Deuteronomy 19:11—"rises up against him"—is the second. Deuteronomy 28:7 also uses the same expression—"your enemies who rise up against you"—suggesting that Israel's enemies are men like Cain and also God's enemies.

blood is shed, as Abel's was, it cries out to God from the ground, seeking God's righteous judgment (Gen. 4:10). Thus, innocent blood—or, better, the guilt of innocent blood—must be purged from the land.[11]

> But if any man hate his neighbor, and lie in wait for him, and rise up against him, and smite him mortally so that he dieth, and he flee into one of these cities; then the elders of his city shall send and fetch him thence, and deliver him into the hand of the avenger of blood, that he may die. Thine eye shall not pity him, but thou shalt purge the innocent blood from Israel, that it may go well with thee. (Deut. 19:11–13)

If the Israelites judge righteously and obey the teaching of Yahweh's covenant with Noah (Gen. 9:5–6) and Moses' instruction in Deuteronomy by purging the guilt of innocent blood from the land, it will go well with them, for Yahweh their Father will bless them.

Deuteronomy 28:63
The list of curses in the book of Deuteronomy unfolds the passion of Yahweh's fury that would burst against His son if he rebelled. If Israel turns his back on Yahweh, betraying the covenant, then Yahweh will send His son back into slavery. The expression in 28:63 is particularly discomfiting.

---

11. Purging evil from the land is the more common expression (Deut. 13:5; 17:7, 12; 19:19; 21:21; 22:21–22, 24; 24:7), but it has the same basic concern. Sin defiles the land and it must be purged so that Yahweh can continue to bless His people. Deuteronomy 21:1–9 instructs Israel in how to treat a case of unsolvable murder, "So shalt thou purge the innocent blood from the midst of thee, when thou shalt do that which is right in the eyes of Yahweh" (21:9).

> And it shall come to pass, that, as Yahweh rejoiced over you to do you good, and to multiply you, so Yahweh will rejoice over you to cause you to perish, and to destroy you; and ye shall be plucked from off the land whither thou goest in to possess it. (Deut. 28:63)

As the Father of the people of Israel, of course Yahweh delighted to do them good. This part of the verse suggests the comfort of Yahweh's Fatherly love. The allusion to the Fifth Word indicates that their relationship to Yahweh as children to a Father is presupposed. The expression "rejoiced to . . . multiply you" alludes to the Abrahamic covenant. Two of the most profound images of blessing and well-being are referred to. But the comfort suggested in these expressions is immediately erased when we discover that if the Israelites turn away from Yahweh, then He will delight equally much in their destruction, a terrifying prospect. Whenever we read of Israel in a time of apostasy, they do not seem to even consider the possibility that they could so offend their Lord that He would delight to destroy them, even though they were warned of it from the beginning.

Deuteronomy 30:5
In Deuteronomy 28:63 and 30:5, the allusion to the Fifth Word is somewhat less clear, since the language is not "it will go well with you," but "as Yahweh rejoiced over you to do you good" (28:63), and "Yahweh thy God . . . will do thee good . . ." (30:5). But it is the same verb (יטב) that is used in the Fifth Word, only the tense is different, indicating that "it will go well" because Yahweh will "cause it to go well," or "do thee good," or "prosper thee."

> Yahweh thy God will bring thee into the land which thy fathers possessed, and thou shalt possess it; and he will do thee good, and multiply thee above thy fathers. (Deut. 30:5)

The context of this promise in Deuteronomy 30 begins in verse 1 where Moses speaks of all the curses of the covenant being realized and Israel being carried away into a foreign land. In other words, the children of Israel will once again experience something like Egyptian bondage (30:1). As in the days of Moses, they will cry out unto Yahweh for deliverance and He will hear them (30:2-3). So Yahweh will bring them back into the land to do them good (30:5).

The promise to "multiply" them alludes to the Abrahamic covenant in Genesis 12 and related passages. It is associated with the promise of long life and well-being in Deuteronomy, so that it fits in with the Father/son covenant theme. The fact that in Genesis the command to multiply begins with God's son Adam is probably related. Adam was created to be like God. The command to multiply and fill the earth was a commission that called for him to fulfill the God-created potential of his nature. Since he failed, that task eventually was given to Abraham and his seed. When Deuteronomy speaks of the multiplication of the children of Israel and associates it with the Father/son relationship, Moses apparently regards Israel as a new creation.

Conclusion

I have listed seven allusions to the first promise and another eight allusions to the second promise of the Fifth Word. This is quite a significant number of allusions. But as our brief survey has shown, it is not just a matter of quantity. Allusions to the promises of the

Fifth Word occur in some of the most important passages of Deuteronomy and they are associated with the most fundamental obligations of the covenant. Not only the frequency of allusion to the Fifth Word, but also the quality of the allusions establishes the Father/son relationship as the basic covenant metaphor in Deuteronomy.

As I pointed out, however, there is a complication. The Father/son relationship in Deuteronomy is not necessarily a successful relationship. Love is a two-way street and there are obligations of love for the son. However much the Father loves and pleads with the son, the son must respond in love for the relationship to stand. In addition to the Fatherly love of Yahweh, Deuteronomy also speaks of the rebellious son who must be cast out. This adds another dimension to the consideration of Yahweh's covenant with Israel.

Chapter Four

The Rebellious Son

Just as allusions to the Fifth Word in passages about Yahweh's relationship with the children of Israel have not received due attention, allusions to the law of the rebellious son have often been quite neglected. For example, P. C. Cragie and J. A. Thompson, both of whom have written helpful commentaries on Deuteronomy, seem not to recognize that within Deuteronomy the law of the rebellious son is an important theme that defines Israel's relationship with God.[1] Duane L. Christensen refers to Israel acting as a rebellious son in the covenant history recorded in later books of the Old Testament, but he does not seem to appreciate the intertextual references to the rebellious son within Deuteronomy.[2]

---

1. See P. C. Cragie, *The Book of Deuteronomy* (Grand Rapids: Eerdmans, 1976), 283–85, and J. A. Thompson, *Deuteronomy* (Downers Grove, IL: Inter-Varsity, 1976), 230–32.

2. See Duane L. Christensen, *Deuteronomy 21:10–34:12* (Nashville: Thomas Nelson, 2002), 480–85.

I argue that the original audience would have noticed Moses' allusions to the rebellious son, in part because the Father/son covenant metaphor, introduced in Exodus 4:22, is given a prominent place in Deuteronomy. For the congregation in Moses' day, the rich web of allusion to the Fifth Word and the references to Yahweh as Israel's Father would inescapably come to mind when they read the law of the rebellious son, for Moses makes explicit allusion to the Law through key words and phrases.

Of course, it is possible to construe the relationship the other way. The law of the rebellious son may be alluding to the children of Israel in the wilderness. Chronologically, that would be the more logical way to view the matter. In terms of the flow of Deuteronomy, Israel's rebelliousness is referred to a number of times before the law itself is stated in Deuteronomy 21:18–21, so it might be preferable to see the law as alluding to the history. However, the fuller statement of the rebellion of the son, and the key words defining the rebellious son who is worthy of death, come with the law of the rebellious son. It is these expressions that provide the literary links to create the web of allusion.

From the beginning of Deuteronomy, Israel's history is related in a manner that evokes the metaphor of the rebellious son. Yahweh had redeemed His firstborn son from Egypt, but the son rebelled against Yahweh in the desert, and not just once. A final act of apostasy provoked the death penalty on the generation that left Egypt. Thus, the history of the first generation is too obviously the history of a son so rebellious that he had to be punished severely. This is repeatedly reflected upon in Deuteronomy in language that recalls the law of the rebellious son. Moreover, Moses knew that Israel's history of rebellion would be repeated in the future (Deut. 31:27–29).

The law of the rebellious son provided key terms that defined what kind of a son Israel was and tragically would continue to be. The importance of this intertextual network is seen by the fact that other writers of ancient Scripture picked up on Moses' allusion and drew attention to Israel's rebelliousness in accordance with the Mosaic paradigm.

The Law of the Rebellious Son

Let's begin our consideration of this aspect of the Father/son metaphor by looking at the law of the rebellious son.

> If a man have a stubborn and rebellious son, that will not obey the voice of his father, or the voice of his mother, and, though they chasten him, will not hearken unto them; then shall his father and his mother lay hold on him, and bring him out unto the elders of his city, and unto the gate of his place; and they shall say unto the elders of his city, This our son is stubborn and rebellious, he will not obey our voice; he is a glutton, and a drunkard. And all the men of his city shall stone him to death with stones: so shalt thou put away the evil from the midst of thee; and all Israel shall hear, and fear. (Deut. 21:18–21)

Key Expressions

One of the remarkable features of this law is the way key words and phrases are repeated in a short paragraph. Ancient people, hearing the law read aloud, could hardly miss this aspect of the law. These words and phrases, appearing in another context, would almost certainly prompt readers and hearers to recall the law of the rebellious son. The most obvious, of course, is the expression "stubborn and rebellious son." Within the law itself it is repeated twice, perhaps suggesting its broader significance. If the exact expression is not common and it occurred in another context, the literary link would be established beyond reasonable doubt. Similar expressions or variations on this expression would serve the same function. For example, use of either of the key words "rebellious" or "stubborn" in a context speaking of Israel as God's son would be an unmistakable allusion.

Another expression repeated here in this law is "will not obey the voice." In the first instance, the exact expression is "will not obey the voice of his father or the voice of his mother" (21:18) and in the second, it is "will not obey our voice" (21:20). If Deuteronomy includes passages that speak of not obeying Yahweh's voice, especially if the passage occurs in a context which alludes to the Father/son relationship, an allusion to the law of the rebellious son would be clear.

The expression "though they chasten him, will not hearken" is not repeated, but it is close to the expression "will not obey the voice" and is a key expression in the law. Also, references to chastening obviously presuppose a Father/son relationship. In a context in which the chastening is unsuccessful, this law would almost certainly be recalled.

Allusions Outside of Deuteronomy
If Moses is alluding to the law of the rebellious son within Deuteronomy, we might expect that other ancient writers would notice this. After all, I am arguing that this is a self-conscious literary device on the part of Moses that was intended to communicate to the people of his time. It would be odd if no other ancient writer noticed what Moses was doing. An important aspect of demonstrating an allusion here is evidence

from ancient writers that indicates they saw such an allusion.

We will look, therefore, for two sorts of evidence. First, we will search within Deuteronomy for key words or phrases, especially in contexts that speak of the Father/son relationship. Second, we consider the question of whether or not Israel's prophets or poets show evidence of understanding Moses' allusions to the law of the rebellious son. If the answer to this were negative, my thesis might still stand, but it would not seem vital for understanding God's relationship with Israel. If, however, there is weighty evidence for the metaphor of the rebellious son outside of Deuteronomy alluding back to Moses, then we have good grounds for assuming this is a fundamental aspect of Moses' final sermon to Israel and of the self-understanding of a godly Israelite.

The Rebellious Son in Deuteronomy

The key word "stubborn" (סרר) only appears in Deuteronomy in 21:18, 20, and only seventeen times in the entire Old Testament (Deut. 21:18, 20; Isa. 1:23; 30:1; 65:2; Jer. 5:23; 6:28; Hos. 4:16; 9:15; Zech. 7:11; Psa. 66:7; 68:6, 18; 78:8; Prov. 7:11; Neh. 9:29.). Its relatively rare occurrence outside of Deuteronomy makes literary links with the law of the rebellious son easily identifiable.[3] Within Deuteronomy, other words and expressions create a network of allusions. In particular, the key words "rebellious"[4] (מרה) and "discipline" (יסר), and the

---

3. We will discuss references outside of Deuteronomy in the next section.
4. In Deuteronomy 21:18, 20, where the word occurs two times, the verb appears as a participle מוֹרֶה, hence it is translated "rebellious."

expression "hearken unto the voice" (שְׁמַע בְּ קוֹל) stand out.

Rebellious (מרה)

The Hebrew word "rebellious" (מרה) occurs forty-four times in the Old Testament.[5] It appears eight times in the book of Deuteronomy (Deut. 1:26, 43; 9:7, 23–24; 21:18, 20; 31:27), two of which, of course, are in the law of the rebellious son. Only the book of Psalms, in which מרה occurs ten times, has more occurrences of this word. Each reference in Deuteronomy deserves brief attention.

The first reference in Deuteronomy 1:26 appears in an important context—Moses' assertion that God carried Israel in the wilderness as a father carries his son. Moses begins by recounting the story of the spies being sent into Canaan and reminds them that the spies all reported that the land was good (Deut. 1:25). The report of the ten spies about the strength of the Canaanites which filled the children of Israel with fear is not repeated here, only the unbelieving response.

> Yet ye would not go up, but rebelled against the commandment of Yahweh your God ... (Deut. 1:26)

The children of Israel expressed their rebellion, "It is because the LORD hates us that he has brought us out of the land of Egypt, to hand us over to the Amorites to destroy us" (1:27). Moses answered them.

---

5. It is used forty-four times in forty-three verses (Num 20:10, 24; 27:14; Deut. 1:26, 43; 9:7, 23–24; 21:18, 20; 31:27; Josh. 1:18; 1 Sam. 12:14–15; 1 Kings 13:21, 26; 2 Kings 14:26; Isa. 1:20; 3:8; 50:5; 63:10; Jer. 4:17; 5:23; Ezek. 5:6; 20:8, 13, 21; Hos. 13:16; Ps. 5:10; 78:8, 17, 40, 56; 105:28; 106:7, 33, 43; 107:11; Job 17:2; Lam. 1:18, 20; 3:42; Neh. 9:26), including two times in Lamentations 1:20.

> Dread not, neither be afraid of them. Yahweh your God who goeth before you, he will fight for you, according to all that he did for you in Egypt before your eyes, and in the wilderness, where thou hast seen how that Yahweh thy God bare thee, as a man doth bear his son, in all the way that ye went, until ye came unto this place. (Deut. 1:29-31)

The story of Israel's unbelief continues as Moses recounts their waywardness, again using the key word "rebellion" (מרה) to describe their rejection of Yahweh.

> So I spake unto you, and ye hearkened not;[6] but ye rebelled against the commandment of Yahweh, and were presumptuous, and went up into the hill-country. (Deut. 1:43)

Thus, the first two occurrences of the verb form of the word "rebel" (מרה) appear in close proximity with the first reference to the Fatherhood of Yahweh. Moreover, both references are part of Moses' retelling the story of Israel's climactic act of apostasy, which resulted in the death penalty in the wilderness (Deut. 1:19-46; cf. Num. 13-14). Fatherly love, rebellion, and the death penalty appearing together in a single narrative context constitute an unmistakable literary link to the law of the rebellious son.

The next double occurrence of the word "rebel" (מרה) is in an equally significant context, though in this case there is no explicit reference to the children of Israel as Yahweh's son. From Deuteronomy 9:7 to 10:11, Moses reminds the people of Israel of their sinful rebellion against Yahweh. Two particular instances stand out.

---

6. The Hebrew here is not identical to the expression in Deuteronomy 21:18-21, but it is close enough to enforce the allusion already suggested by the use of מרה.

First, the incident which is given most attention is the worship of the golden calf at Mt. Sinai. Second, the climactic act of apostasy at Kadesh-barnea, though treated only briefly, is given emphasis (9:23–24).

Just before this long recitation of Israel's sin, in the verse immediately preceding, Moses describes Israel's stubbornness using an expression that is synonymous with the word for "stubborn" in 21:18.

> Know therefore, that Yahweh thy God giveth thee not this good land to possess it for thy righteousness; for thou art a stiff-necked people. (Deut. 9:6)

Thus, Deuteronomy 9:6 prepares the way for 9:7–10:11 by using an important expression for Israel's rebellion, one which is repeated soon. Moreover, Deuteronomy 9:6 and 9:13 are allusions to the book of Exodus, in which the expression קְשֵׁה־עֹרֶף (stiff-necked) occurs four times (Ex. 32:9; 33:3, 5; 34:9), all related to the incident of the idolatrous worship of the golden calf at Mt. Sinai. Since the history in 9:7–10:11 concentrates on the incident at Sinai, this expression appears at the beginning.

When Moses actually begins to recite the history, however, he switches to the word for rebellion used of the rebellious son, מרה.

> Remember, forget thou not, how thou provokedst Yahweh thy God to wrath in the wilderness: from the day that thou wentest forth out of the land of Egypt, until ye came unto this place, ye have been rebellious against Yahweh. (Deut. 9:7)

To help them remember, Moses tells the story of the rebellion at Mt. Sinai and includes allusions to other instances of rebellion as well, but he puts it all together in an interesting fashion. The other instances of rebellion are inserted into the ongoing story of the account of Sinai, as if to say that these other incidents were also examples of idolatry of some sort. It is with reference to these inserted examples of rebellion that there is a clear allusion to the law of the rebellious son.

> And at Taberah, and at Massah, and at Kibroth-hattaavah, ye provoked Yahweh to wrath. And when Yahweh sent you from Kadesh-barnea, saying, Go up and possess the land which I have given you; then ye rebelled against the commandment of Yahweh your God, and ye believed him not, nor hearkened to his voice. Ye have been rebellious against Yahweh from the day that I knew you. (Deut. 9:22–24)

The key word rebellious (מרה), used twice in the law of the rebellious son, appears in this context also twice (9:23, 24). Since the word is used infrequently in Deuteronomy, the link is clear enough. But there is more. In addition to the key word for rebellion, the key expression, "not hearken to the voice" (שמע בְּ קוֹל)—which appears twice in the law of the rebellious son (21:18, 20)—also appears in 9:23. The rebellion of Israel at Mt. Sinai expressed the true heart of Yahweh's foolish and rebellious son, which bore bad fruit in the climactic act of apostasy at Kadesh-barnea, resulting in the sentence of death.

This brings us to the final use of the word מרה, which is also a profoundly significant passage within Deuteronomy.

> Take this book of the law, and put it by the side of the ark of the covenant of Yahweh your God, that it may be there for a witness against thee. For I know thy rebellion (מרי, noun form of מרה) and thy stiff-

neck (עָרְפְּךָ הַקָּשֶׁה, a slightly different form of the same expression occurring in 9:6): behold, while I am yet alive with you this day, ye have been rebellious (מרה) against Yahweh; and how much more after my death? (Deut. 31:26-27)

These verses occur in the introduction to the Song of Moses. There is a threefold repetition of Israel's rebelliousness linking to both the law of the rebellious son and the history of Israel's rebellion at Sinai. The song itself will take up the theme of the rebellious son in other language, but after the repeated allusions earlier in the book, the less direct allusion brings the basic theme to mind. Moses' song includes a poignant restatement of the Father's love and His son's rebellion.

> They have dealt corruptly with him,
> They are not his children,
> It is their blemish;
> They are a perverse and crooked generation.
> Do ye thus requite Yahweh,
> O foolish people and unwise?
> Is not he thy father that hath bought thee?
> He hath made thee, and established thee. (32:5-6)

> Of the Rock that begat thee thou art unmindful,
> And hast forgotten God that gave thee birth.
> And Yahweh saw it, and abhorred them,
> Because of the provocation of his sons and his
>   daughters.
> And he said, I will hide my face from them,
> I will see what their end shall be:
> For they are a very perverse generation,
> Children in whom is no faithfulness. (32:18-20)

In conclusion, the use of the word מרה in Deuteronomy alludes repeatedly to the law of the rebellious son. It testifies to the nature of the whole book. Israel is Yahweh's son whom He redeemed from Egypt, but Israel rebelled against Him. Eventually the son had to be put to death, but, thankfully, that is not the end of the story.

Would Not Listen (אֵינֶנּוּ שֹׁמֵעַ בְּקֹלֵנוּ)

The full expression "not obey the voice" is not used apart from Deuteronomy 21:18 and 20. But there are expressions close enough to constitute allusions to the law of the rebellious son, especially when used in a context that alludes to the Father/son relationship. The most obvious example is Deuteronomy 1:43, since it refers to rebellion and a refusal to listen to Yahweh in the same verse in a context in which Israel is called Yahweh's son. Similarly, though lacking a reference to sonship, Deuteronomy 9:23 seems to be alluding to the law of the rebellious son through the word "rebellious." The added expression "and ye believed him not, nor hearkened to his voice," clarifies the allusion.

Other references in the book of Deuteronomy to not hearing—often translated "not obey"—the command or voice of Yahweh perhaps all echo the law of the rebellious son, since the refusal to listen to Yahweh's voice was Israel's basic sin. Whenever Yahweh warned them, encouraged them, or rebuked them, the essential issue was whether or not Israel would listen to the voice of Yahweh (Deut. 1:43; 8:20; 9:23; 11:28; 13:18; 15:5; 18:19; 26:14, 17; 27:10; 28:1–2, 15, 45, 62; 30:2, 8, 10, 17, 20).

Discipline (יסר)

Even though his father and mother chastised or disciplined him, the rebellious son would not listen. The word for discipline (יסר) is only used four times in the book of Deuteronomy. One occurrence is in a purely judicial context (22:18), but that unites family discipline to judicial discipline. Family discipline is the foundation for social harmony and peace. When it fails, judicial discipline must be applied. In the case of the rebellious son, though he had been disciplined with family love, he refused to listen. The only recourse is to take him to the elders of the gate so that they may apply a judicial sentence.[7] The judgment of the elders takes the discipline of the parents one step further, as it were.

The other two references to "discipline" in the book of Deuteronomy presuppose the Father/son relationship between Yahweh and Israel (4:36; 8:5) and one of them is quite explicit (8:5). Neither passage alludes to the rebellious son. However, in the larger narrative context of Deuteronomy, we see that though Yahweh disciplined Israel in the wilderness, His son was stubborn and rebellious, rejecting the word of Yahweh (Deut. 29:4, 24–28; 31:16–21, 26–29).

The Rebellious Son Outside of Deuteronomy

Even one clear allusion to the law of the rebellious son would demonstrate that an ancient reader may have read Deuteronomy with the Father/son/rebellious son covenant metaphor in mind. Of course, it would not be impossible that a later writer created the link himself. Deciding on whether the link was a new idea to a later writer or an allusion to something that Moses was doing depends on the exact language of the allusion to the

---

7. Calvin rightly points out that this means a fair trial for the son and examination of the parents as well. This law should not be understood as a harsh method for parents to subdue their children. In fact, we may doubt that it was ever applied. Its literary function was no doubt more important than its social.

law of the rebellious son. I have chosen verses that seem clearly to be picking up on Moses' paradigm.

Isaiah 30:1–2

I begin with an example that seems to constitute an unmistakable allusion to Israel as rebellious children. The relatively rare verb סרר, translated "stubborn" in Deuteronomy 21:18, 20, occurs here.[8] As I pointed out above, "stubborn" is used in Deuteronomy only twice (21:18, 20) and in the rest of the Old Testament only fifteen times (Isa. 1:23; 30:1; 65:2; Jer. 5:23; 6:28; Hos. 4:16 [twice]; 9:15; Zech. 7:11; Psa. 66:7; 68:6, 18; 78:8; Prov. 7:11; Neh. 9:29). Given the relative infrequency of the verb and its exclusive use in Deuteronomy to refer to the rebellious son, we might expect an echo of the law in Deuteronomy to be resonating in the background of every occasion of this verb. But surely the following is obvious.

> Woe to the rebellious children, saith Yahweh,
> that take counsel, but not of me;
> and that make a league, but not of my Spirit,
> that they may add sin to sin,
> that set out to go down into Egypt,
> and have not asked at my mouth;
> to strengthen themselves in the strength of Pharaoh,
> and to take refuge in the shadow of Egypt! (Isa. 30:1–2)

Seeking salvation from Assyria through the help of the Egyptians was analogous to Israel in the wilderness deciding to return to Egypt rather than fight against the

---

8. Sixteen out of the seventeen occurrences of this verb are participial forms (Deut. 21:18, 20; Isa. 1:23; 30:1; 65:2; Jer. 5:23; 6:28; Hos. 4:16; 9:15; Zech. 7:11; Ps. 66:7; 68:6, 18; 78:8; Prov. 7:11; Neh. 9:29). The only exception is the second of two occurrences in Hosea 4:16.

Canaanites. The woe pronounced on the rebellious children clearly recalls the law of the rebellious son, who is beyond mere chastisement. Thus, we find here allusions to Israel's rebellion in the wilderness, as well as to the law of the rebellious son, which means that Isaiah read Deuteronomy in the light of the Father/son covenant love and the law of the rebellious son.

Jeremiah 5:23

Jeremiah also alludes to the law of the rebellious son in language that is unambiguous, though he does not explicitly refer to Judah as Yahweh's son. The allusion is apparent, however, because the language is so rare. The combined expression "stubborn and rebellious" (וּמוֹרֶה סוֹרֵר) occurs only four times in the entire Hebrew Bible, two of which are in Deuteronomy (21:18, 20). Jeremiah 5:23 is one of the other two instances.

> But this people hath a stubborn and rebellious heart;
> they are turned aside and gone away. (Jer. 5:23)

The entire fifth chapter of Jeremiah bewails Judah's disobedience and foolishness. The love of Yahweh for His people and Jeremiah's anguish because of their sin combine with expressions of righteous wrath against idolatry and the inescapable judgment to come. The allusion to the law of the rebellious son expresses the frustration of Yahweh at Judah's rebellion and the righteousness of the penalty.

Psalm 78:8

Similarly Psalm 78:8, the only other passage in the Old Testament to use the exact expression "stubborn and rebellious" (סוֹרֵר וּמוֹרֶה), borrows the language of the law in Deuteronomy 21:18, 20, when it refers to a "a stubborn and rebellious generation." Here the psalmist is describing the first generation of the children of Israel who came out of Egypt, indicating that he notes and repeats Moses' literary device.

> For he established a testimony in Jacob,
> And appointed a law in Israel,
> Which he commanded our fathers,
> That they should make them known to their children;
> That the generation to come might know them,
> even the children that should be born;
> Who should arise and tell them to their children,
> That they might set their hope in God,
> And not forget the works of God,
> But keep his commandments,
> And might not be as their fathers,
> A stubborn and rebellious generation,
> A generation that set not their heart aright,
> And whose spirit was not steadfast with
> God. (Psa. 78:5–8)

Of course, literary allusion is not limited to establishing a connection to what has been stated before. Allusion not only places two texts side by side, it may also "play" with the prior text, sometimes revising, sometimes seeming to contradict, sometimes adding new perspective. In this way, allusion broadens our perspective on an issue and forces us to meditate on the text.

Here in Psalm 78, just as in Deuteronomy, the psalmist explicitly identifies the first generation as rebellious. Also, in Psalm 78, there is clearly a concern about generational faithfulness (cf. 5–8); the fathers are to teach their children to follow Israel's God. But there is an ironic twist. The psalmist speaks of "fathers" who are "a stubborn and rebellious generation," alluding to Deuteronomy 21:18–21, which addresses the problem of rebellious "sons."

Thus, Psalm 78:8 borrows the language of Deuteronomy and puts it into a song that reminds the Israelites of the rebellion of the first generation, the fathers. In the context, the father/son relationship stands out so emphatically that an allusion to "stubborn and rebellious" *fathers* must be intentional irony. So, also, in the original law, it was the son who was a glutton and drunkard, but in Psalm 78, it is the *fathers* in the wilderness who are gluttons (78:18 ff.).[9]

The fact that Psalm 78 can allude to the law in this ironic fashion suggests that the Psalmist understood the rebellious-son paradigm in the book of Deuteronomy and appropriated it from a somewhat different perspective to enforce the lesson for the people of his own day. His dependence on Deuteronomy is clear, but it is also clear that he shifts from sons to fathers in order to shock his readers into self-awareness. Moses had said directly to the Israelites of his day that God did not choose them because of their righteousness, for they had always been a rebellious people (Deut. 9:4–5ff.). The psalmist, speaking to a later generation, said don't be like your rebellious *fathers* that died in the wilderness because they were worthless sons of Yahweh who would not hear His word—a shocking message for people who held fathers in great respect.

Zechariah 7:11

In Zechariah it is the key word "stubborn" (סרר) that appears. However, there are also references to the people of Israel not listening (cf. Deut. 21:18). Though the

---

9. Note also that Psalm 78 repeatedly uses the other Hebrew word that describes the rebellious son—מרה (Ps 78:17, 40, 56).

exact words of the law in Deuteronomy are not used, the ideas seem parallel. Together with the use of the key word "stubborn," a reference to "not listening," resulting in something like a death penalty, supports the idea that Zechariah alludes to the law of the rebellious son. The entire brief oracle is worth quoting.

> Thus hath Yahweh of hosts spoken, saying, Execute true judgment, and show kindness and compassion every man to his brother; and oppress not the widow, nor the fatherless, the sojourner, nor the poor; and let none of you devise evil against his brother in your heart. But they refused to hearken, and turned a stubborn (סרר) shoulder, and stopped their ears, that they might not hear. Yea, they made their hearts as an adamant stone, lest they should hear the law, and the words which Yahweh of hosts had sent by his Spirit by the former prophets: Therefore there came great wrath from Yahweh of hosts. And it is come to pass that, as he cried, and they would not hear, so they shall cry, and I will not hear, said Yahweh of hosts; but I will scatter them with a whirlwind among all the nations which they have not known. Thus the land was desolate after them, so that no man passed through nor returned: for they laid the pleasant land desolate. (Zech. 7:9–14)

Nehemiah 9:29
Like the reference in Zechariah, the allusion in Nehemiah depends largely on the key word "stubborn" (סרר) in the phrase "turned a stubborn shoulder." Again, there is a reference to Israel "not hearing" God's Word and the resultant penalty of death for their sin. Though in

Zechariah and Nehemiah, the echo may be faint, it is not absent, since the key word סרר is so rare.[10]

> But after they had rest, they did evil again before thee; therefore leftest thou them in the hand of their enemies, so that they had the dominion over them: yet when they returned, and cried unto thee, thou heardest from heaven; and many times didst thou deliver them according to thy mercies, and testifiedst against them, that thou mightest bring them again unto thy law. Yet they dealt proudly, and hearkened not unto thy commandments, but sinned against thine ordinances, which if a man do, he shall live in them, and turned a stubborn (סרר) shoulder, and hardened their neck, and would not hear. Yet many years didst thou bear with them, and testifiedst against them by thy Spirit through thy prophets: yet would they not give ear: therefore gavest thou them into the hand of the peoples of the lands. (Neh. 9:28-30)

1 Samuel 12:14-15

As I pointed out above, the Hebrew word translated "rebellious" is much more common than the word translated "stubborn," but in a context which speaks of "hearken unto the voice," another key expression from Deuteronomy 21:18, the literary link seems relatively clear.

> If ye will fear Yahweh, and serve him, and hearken unto his voice, and not rebel against the commandment of Yahweh, and both ye and also the king that

---

10. Another word referring to rebellion (סָרָה) is probably related to סרר. It occurs only seven times in the entire Hebrew Bible and usually expresses rebellion that deserves the death penalty (Deut. 13:5; 19:16; Isa 1:5; 31:6; 59:13; Jer 28:16; 29:32).

reigneth over you be followers of Yahweh your God, it will be well: but if ye will not hearken unto the voice of Yahweh, but rebel against the commandment of Yahweh, then will the hand of Yahweh be against you, as it was against your fathers. (1 Sam. 12:14–15)

It is true that the expression "hearken to the voice" (קוֹל בְּ שָׁמַע) is a common one.[11] But it is seldom used in the same context with מרה (rebellious). In fact, outside of Deuteronomy, this combination appears only in two verses—1 Samuel 12:14–15. Of the other three occurrences, two are in the law of the rebellious son (Deut. 18:18, 20). Add to this an allusion to the Fifth Word's promise in the words "it will be well" and the literary link is apparent. Samuel is self-consciously speaking to the people of Israel in his day as Moses spoke to the people of Israel in a previous generation.

Numbers 20:10, 24; 27:14

The most surprising instances of the word מרה outside of Deuteronomy occur *before* Deuteronomy in the book of Numbers. Numbers chapter 20 records the sinful rebellion and unbelief of two leaders who are condemned to die in the wilderness for their sin. They are the first men in the Bible specifically identified by this Hebrew

---

11. It appears eighty times in the Hebrew Bible (Gen. 21:12; 22:18; 27:8, 13, 43; 30:6; Ex. 4:1; 5:2; 18:19; 19:5; 23:21–22; Num. 14:22; Deut. 4:30; 9:23; 13:18; 15:5; 21:18, 20; 26:14, 17; 27:10; 28:1–2, 15, 45, 62; 30:2, 8, 10, 20; Josh. 5:6; 22:2; Judg. 2:2; 6:10; 20:13; 1 Sam. 8:7, 9, 19, 22; 12:1, 14–15; 15:19–20, 22, 24; 25:35; 28:18; 2 Sam. 12:18; 13:14; 1 Kings 20:36; 2 Kings 18:12; Isa. 50:10; Jer. 3:25; 7:23, 28; 9:13; 11:4, 7; 18:10; 22:21; 26:13; 32:23; 35:8; 40:3; 42:6, 13, 21; 43:7; 44:23; Zeph. 3:2; Psa. 26:7; 103:20; 106:25; Prov. 5:13; Dan. 9:10–11, 14; 2 Chr. 30:27).

word and their sin won for them the death penalty in the wilderness.

In their anger, Moses and Aaron shouted at the people of Israel, "Hear now, ye rebels (מרה); shall we bring you forth water out of this rock?" This is the first use of the word in the entire Old Testament, but it is followed soon after in the narrative describing Moses and Aaron.

> And Yahweh said unto Moses and Aaron, Because ye believed not in me, to sanctify me in the eyes of the children of Israel, therefore ye shall not bring this assembly into the land which I have given them. (20:12)

> And Yahweh spake unto Moses and Aaron in mount Hor, by the border of the land of Edom, saying, Aaron shall be gathered unto his people; for he shall not enter into the land which I have given unto the children of Israel, because ye rebelled (מרה) against my word at the waters of Meribah. (20:23–24)

The word appears again in Numbers 27 when Yahweh tells Moses that he must die in the wilderness like his brother Aaron.

> And when thou hast seen it, thou also shalt be gathered unto thy people, as Aaron thy brother was gathered; because ye rebelled against my word in the wilderness of Zin, in the strife of the congregation, to sanctify me at the waters before their eyes. These are the waters of Meribah of Kadesh in the wilderness of Zin. (27:14)

Unbelief and rebellion against Yahweh's word was the sin that the whole nation committed at Kadesh-barnea, the sin for which they had to die in the wilderness. The profound irony is that Moses and Aaron, in the very last year of the wilderness wandering, only a few months away from the time they would have entered the land, imitated the sin of the nation and brought upon themselves the same punishment as the rest of the first generation. When, therefore, Moses in Deuteronomy refers to Israel's sin in the wilderness and her tendency to rebel, we should not read his words as harsh or condemnatory. Moses wrote as a sinner writing to sinners to win them to repentance.

Conclusion
There are other references to support the conclusion that writers after Moses noted the language of Deuteronomy and alluded to the law of the rebellious son, but what has been offered above is sufficient to demonstrate that ancient writers saw this covenant metaphor. It is not the invention of someone overly enthusiastic about intertextuality.

There is, however, a legitimate question about which is referring to which. Is the law of the rebellious son an allusion to the children of Israel's rebellion in the wilderness, a law given to Israel just before they entered the land to remind them of what they have done and why the first generation had to die? Or, are the references to the children of Israel's rebellion in Deuteronomy intentionally couched in the language of the law of the rebellious son in order to draw a parallel? Perhaps it is not necessary to make a choice here. However we answer this question, the story of Israel's rebellion and the law of the rebellious son are intimately linked, not only in the book of Deuteronomy, but in the religious consciousness of later writers of Scripture.

Finally, it is important to note—and to emphasize—that Deuteronomy does not end with the rebellious son. If it did, it might indeed sound something like a covenant of works. If the rebellious son were the final perspective, we might read the law as if its last word for the people of Israel was a word of condemnation. But it is not. Just as the first word for Israel is Yahweh's gracious call of Abraham, so the last word is Yahweh's gracious promise that He will someday give them a new heart, so that the nation will return to Him. The final word in Deuteronomy, literally Moses' last words, is the word of love and blessing.[12]

Let me elaborate briefly on these two points. First, Moses does give hope to the children of Israel, even though his song was so full of the rebellious son motif. The words of encouragement and hope come before the song, thereby qualifying the song's references to rebellion. Reading—and singing—the Song of Moses in the light of the previous promise of salvation means that one reads the verses about Israel's rebelliousness as intended to prompt the repentance that will lead to restoration. The promise is the frame for the song.

> And it shall come to pass, when all these things are come upon thee, the blessing and the curse, which I have set before thee, and thou shalt call them to mind among all the nations, whither Yahweh thy God hath driven thee, and shalt return unto Yahweh thy God, and shalt obey his voice according to all that I command thee this day, thou and thy children, with all thy heart, and with all thy soul; that then Yahweh thy God will turn thy captivity, and have compassion upon thee, and will return and gather thee from all the peoples, whither Yahweh

---

12. I believe that our Lord Himself alludes to this in the parable of the prodigal son, which can be described as a parabolic depiction of the covenant between gracious Yahweh and His foolish son, Israel. Like Deuteronomy, Jesus' parable ends with love and grace for the sinners who repent.

> thy God hath scattered thee. If any of thine outcasts be in the uttermost parts of heaven, from thence will Yahweh thy God gather thee, and from thence will he fetch thee: and Yahweh thy God will bring thee into the land which thy fathers possessed, and thou shalt possess it; and he will do thee good, and multiply thee above thy fathers. And Yahweh thy God will circumcise thy heart, and the heart of thy seed, to love Yahweh thy God with all thy heart, and with all thy soul, that thou mayest live. (Deut. 30:1–6)

Second, if there were any doubt that the Song of Moses is to be sung with the previous promise in mind, it must be removed when we take sufficient note of Deuteronomy 33, the very last words of Moses.[13] For the book of Deuteronomy concludes with a chapter in which Moses pronounces blessing on the twelve tribes. Chapter 33 of Deuteronomy has very few expressions that can be made ambiguous and many that are stated in the language of pure blessing. The book therefore does not conclude with the dark message of Israel's past and future disobedience, but with words of blessing and hope, speaking of Yahweh's love and Israel's happiness.

> Yea, he loveth the people. (Deut. 33:3)

> The eternal God is thy dwelling-place,
> And underneath are the everlasting arms.
> And he thrust out the enemy from before thee,
> And said, Destroy.
> And Israel dwelleth in safety,
> The fountain of Jacob alone,
> In a land of grain and new wine;

---

13. Chapter 34 records the death of Moses and Israel's mourning; there are no more words of Moses after the blessing of chapter 33.

Yea, his heavens drop down dew.
Happy art thou, O Israel:
Who is like unto thee, a people saved by Yahweh,
The shield of thy help,
And the sword of thy excellency!
And thine enemies shall submit themselves unto
    thee;
And thou shalt tread upon their high places.
(Deut. 33:27–29)

Chapter Five

The Covenant of the Father and the Son

In this chapter, I want to consider very briefly something of the history and the theology of the covenant in Scripture. In so doing, I will also offer a view on the covenant in ancient Israel and its relationship to covenants and treaties in the Ancient Near East.

Deuteronomy in Critical Scholarship

To investigate the history of the covenant idea, one must have some notion of the chronology of the Ancient Near East. Since the late nineteenth century, most Old Testament scholars have followed J. Wellhausen's documentary hypothesis or one of its modified forms, which presupposes the Bible can be divided up into various source documents identifiable through hints in the text. In the classic view, there are four sources; Jahwist, Elohist, Deuteronomist, and Priestly (JEDP). Jahwist is the oldest source. Israel's religion on this view gradually evolves to become more formalized, with the contributions of the Elohist and Deuteronimist authors. Finally a priestly author or authors add priestly portions. Deuteronomy, on this view, is not a product of Moses, nor does it give guidelines for Israel during most of her history. Rather it comes late in Judah's history, probably at the time of Josiah. Clearly for scholars beginning with this hypothesis, the analysis of the history of the covenant idea and covenant documents in Israel and the Ancient Near East will be largely determined by presuppositions about the evolution of Israel's religion rather than the testimony of the text itself.

But since the 1970s, according to Gordon Wenham, in a slightly-dated but still relevant article on the state of Pentateuchal studies, the question of a paradigm for Old Testament scholarship has become problematic. Wenham demonstrates that there is no scholarly consensus on the composition of the Pentateuch,[1] dividing the theoretical approaches into four groups: "the radical-sceptical, the Jewish critical, the New Critical, and the theological models."[2] There are further divisions within these groups. The bottom line is that modern Old Testament scholarship cannot really offer an answer to questions about the history of the covenant idea, the composition of Deuteronomy, or similar questions. Or, rather, it offers so many conflicting answers that it is of little help.[3]

It is important to stress this because scholars addressing a general audience often speak as if there were a

---

1. Gordon Wenham, "Pentateuchal Studies Today," *Themelios* 22.1 (October 1996), 3–13.

2. Ibid, 4.

3. Writing in 1985, Wenham wrote, "The last decade has been one of great turmoil in the field of documentary studies. Many of the most cherished ideas of the classic documentary theory have been put in serious question by mainline critical scholars." "The Date of Deuteronomy: Linch-pin of Old Testament Criticism. Part One," *Themelios* 10.3 (April 1985), 15.

consensus, as if the "results" of scholarship present us with something like facts that must be taken into account. The utter lack of consensus, either in terms of literary interpretation, history, or theological understanding, undermines the authority of the whole discipline of Old Testament scholarship as it is practiced in the academy. Thus, contrary to what they are told, evangelicals who take the witness of the text at face value do not confront "the problem of the Old Testament," but "the problem of Old Testament scholarship."[4]

> "If it ain't broke, don't fix it" is good advice. But if it is broke, something needs to be done about it. The "it" here is the Documentary Hypothesis as a solution to problems in the Pentateuch. The problems are still there; the Documentary Hypothesis is no longer solving them. A fix is needed.[5]

What was originally not broken—the Pentateuch— the Documentary Hypothesis attempted to fix, with the result that both respect for Scripture and effort to understand the text of the canon declined, as scholars instead formulated ever more ingenious permutations and corrections of the Documentary Hypothesis. Wenham has an excellent expression for the present state of Pentateuchal scholarship: "Rendtorff's dictum." [E]very dating of pentateuchal sources rests on purely hypothetical assumptions.[6]

---

4. Contrary to the view of Peter Enns in *Inspiration and Incarnation: Evangelicals and the Problem of the Old Testament* (Grand Rapids: Baker, 2005).

5. Antony F. Cambell and Mark A. Obrien, *Rethinking the Pentateuch: Prolegomena to the Theology of Ancient Israel* (Louisville: Westminster, John Knox Press, 2005), 1.

6. Wenham, *Themelio*, 15.

Perhaps "purely hypothetical" here should be translated "purely arbitrary." For it is a matter of fact that the Biblical text as it stands offers a more coherent picture of Israel's ancient history, fits well with the archeological evidence we have at the present time, and, when understood in the light of its own chronology, accords with the larger picture of the Ancient Near East we see in the book of Genesis.

To believe that Moses is basically responsible for Deuteronomy[7] offers a coherent picture of ancient Israelite history. Such things as the institution of the prophetic office, the celebration of festivals, the ambiguous designation of the place of central worship, the expressed care for the Levites and the priests, and the laws for dwelling in the land are all not only appropriate, but quite necessary at the time shortly before Moses' death. The people of Israel are about to cross the Jordan and enter the Promised Land, so they need a new explanation of the Law that will focus more particularly on how they are to live once they enter the land. The tabernacle will not be traveling constantly after the conquest, so they need new instruction concerning worship. Also, laws concerning the priesthood and the Levites become relevant in a new way once the people of Israel enter the land, so a new explanation of those laws is important.[8] Given the uniqueness of the time in Israel's history and the fact that Israel is already a literary people, it would be odd in the extreme if in

---

7. He obviously did not write chapter 34 and other minor editorial changes might have been introduced by a prophet like Ezra.

8. Note, for example, the changes in the law about the priests' portion of the sacrifice in Deuteronomy 18:3. No longer living all together as they did in the wilderness means the people of Israel need new laws about animal sacrifice (Deut. 12:15; cf. Lev. 17:3–4) that have implications for the priests. The added portion in Deuteronomy 18:3 presupposes the new law of 12:15.

Moses' day a book like Deuteronomy were not given to Israel. Without it, how would they have understood how to live in the new situation?

There is also the witness of archaeology—though archaeological evidence is problematic at best. On the one hand, it opens new vistas. On the other hand, it can always only be partial. Very little of the material culture of any society remains for archaeologists to dig up, and archaeologists have certainly not found all there is to find. The witness of archaeology, therefore, while fascinating, must be taken with a grain of salt.

Keeping that in mind, K. Kitchen, among others, has shown that the book of Deuteronomy is written in a manner that fits well the pattern of Ancient Near Eastern history in the second millennium BC.[9] Although I differ from those that understand Moses to be appropriating the treaty form that was common in his time, the covenant forms common in Moses' day are not irrelevant to the understanding of Deuteronomy. For example, to the degree that we can find help from archaeology, at this point in time the evidence points clearly to composition in the time of Moses, not at the time suggested, and passionately believed, by the proponents of the modern critical view.

The real issue, however, is Biblical chronology.[10] Nothing is more embarrassing to Christians in the modern world than the fact that the Bible actually presents us with a chronology that contradicts the supposedly solid and certain results of the scientific study of our planet. Scientific study of earth history, including

---

9. Kenneth A. Kitchen, "The Fall and Rise of Covenant, Law and Treaty," *Tyndale Bulletin* 40.1 (1989), 118–35. Meredith Kline's work, which Kitchen refers to, argues along the same lines.

10. See James B. Jordan's writings at http://www.biblicalhorizons.com/category/biblical-chronology/

disciplines like paleontology, geology, and biology, leads modern men to view the planet as very, very old. But the Bible creates a problem for those who would follow its teaching by presenting a chronology of the world that is surprisingly abbreviated—only about 6000 years from the beginning of time until our day. If we take that chronology seriously, our picture of the world is profoundly different from the view of most of our contemporaries.[11]

Deuteronomy in the world of the Bible

If we were to take Biblical chronology and history seriously—which almost all Christians have done until the late nineteenth century—how would we understand Deuteronomy? I am not asking how people in past ages understood Deuteronomy. It is not my aim to turn back the clock. My question is how should a twenty-first-century century Christian understand Deuteronomy without either denying Biblical chronology and history or rejecting what we have learned about the Ancient Near East and ancient history? Obviously to put all the pieces of the puzzle together would require more than a little ingenuity and I do not claim to have the answers. If I had to account for details, I am afraid my best efforts would resemble more the work of Procrustes than Solomon, so I won't make the attempt. But if we take the Bible as our standard, drawing a *general* picture should not be too difficult.

---

11. The arguments against Biblical chronology from the perspective of modern science have answers that satisfy the criteria of scientific explanation, but they do not fit with the presuppositions of most scientists in our day. For a scientist who shows how a young earth is scientifically possible, see John Byl, *God and Cosmos* (Edinburgh: The Banner of Truth Trust, 2001).

Chronology, Babel, and Noah

The first point to be stressed is that there is a growing gap in the academic consensus about Ancient Near Eastern Chronology. The problems in the field of ancient chronology are many and diverse. Peter James offers a description of the situation that indicates how widespread the impact of the chronological question is.

> Over the last century chronology has provided the focus of some of the most protracted and troublesome debates in a wide variety of fields, from European prehistory to biblical archaeology. All these can now be seen as the product of a common cause—a misplaced faith in the immutability of the established framework. The resulting Dark Ages and all their ramifications really amount to a gigantic academic blunder, perpetuated by the convenience of a seemingly reliable time-scale, as well as the sheer complexity of the issues involved. Our investigation shows that these controversies have been largely unnecessary. With the lower chronology proposed here, many simply disappear, along with the illusory Centuries of Darkness.[12]

Of course, James and his colleagues are not suggesting that we turn to the Bible for a reliable chronology of the ancient world. My point in quoting James is just to indicate that when Christians favor the Bible's chronology over other suggested chronologies of the ancient world, it is not like they are denying the sun shines. Though much of academia resists the criticism of James

---

12. Peter James, *Centuries of Darkness: A Challenge to the Conventional Chronology of Old World Archaeology* (New Brunswick, NJ: Rutgers University Press, 1993), 320. There is an internet site devoted to continuing research and debate on the topic at http://www.centuries.co.uk/

and his colleagues, there is no question that a paradigm shift in ancient chronology is on the horizon. Given the present state of academic confusion, the Bible's chronology is certainly worth reconsidering.

In a Biblical chronology of the world, one of the most important issues is that only a few hundred years before Abraham, the world was flooded and reduced to a single family. All the ancient peoples and their cultures descended from Noah. It was only a short time from the flood to the tower of Babel, though an exact chronology cannot be calculated. What can be exactly known is that Noah's son Shem was still alive in the days of Abraham. In other words, the nature of the pre-flood world—the religious, social, and political conventions of the world from Adam to Noah—could still be learned from a first-hand witness. This means that when Babel was constructed, cultural or religions forms that deviated from Noah's teaching were recent. Noah's worldview still exercised a paradigm-defining religious and social influence at the time of Babel and, through Shem, at least to the time of Abraham.

What was Noah's worldview? Noah's worldview was a covenantal worldview grounded in the covenant that God had originally given to Adam in the Garden and then repeated to Noah after the flood. In other words, Noah viewed himself and the world through the lens of God's covenant. The meaning of his life and the world around him were all defined by the creation covenant that had been renewed with Noah after the global deluge. This is a theological truth that is apparent on the surface of the text, but those who deny Biblical chronology relegate the whole story of Noah to the pre-historic, legendary past. Thinking about the impact that Noah and his sons would have had on the ancient world is not part of the discussion.

But what if we ask the question, what kind of a world would have come about if the Biblical story were true? One thing we can hypothesize is that Noah and his descendants would have thought about the world in terms of covenantal categories. Even when his descendants rejected the true God, the change from covenantal to other categories would presumably take considerable time, because "covenant" was not just an idea. Covenants were the glue that held ancient society together. From Noah's time onward they were established through ceremonies that had religious, social, and political significance. Though we can only speculate, it seems likely enough that the first generation to depart from faith in the true God would substitute other gods in the place of the Creator or add gods alongside the Creator rather than invent a whole new framework for conceiving the world. Changing the gods on the shelf is easier than remaking the shelf and the house around it.

What we know of the ancient world fits well with this hypothesis. Covenantal thinking characterized ancient peoples all over the Ancient Near East in the earliest years for which we have any evidence. Also, it continued for a long time in the Ancient Near East and even in the West. In an article that deals with a wide variety of detailed evidence in Hebrew, Akkadian, Phoenician, Aramaic, Greek, and Latin sources, M. Weinfeld concludes as follows:

> The identity in covenant formulations and idiomatic expressions in Mesopotamia, Syro-Palestine, Anatolia, Greece and Rome seems to point towards

a common origin of the treaty terminology in the ancient world.[13]

Weinfield's detailed survey of covenantal terminology suggests both that there is a common source for covenantal thinking in the ancient world and that the covenant paradigm continued to dominate religious, social, and political thinking for centuries. Fitting this evidence into a Biblical framework, it seems that Noah's impact on his descendants was decisive. Though they rejected Noah's God, when they fashioned new gods and new religions, they did so according to the covenantal framework they inherited from Noah.

In this connection it is important to note that one of the distinctive features of the covenant given to Noah was that, by contrast with Adam, Noah and his descendants were given political responsibility. Thus, the fact that Ancient Near Eastern covenantal forms belong not only to the realm of religion but also law and international treaties are entirely in accord with the Biblical picture. If we take that viewpoint for granted, it is perfectly natural to assume that Noah and his sons taught the ancient world to think covenantally, both in religion and politics. Thus, it is not surprising to learn that when ancient men were driven from Babel and moved to other parts of the world, they continued to think in terms of the covenantal framework they learned from Noah. They filled the old forms with new content, but the forms themselves remained. For anyone who takes the Biblical testimony seriously, it is easy to conclude that the common origin of covenantal thinking that Weinfeld testifies to, which lasted so long in the an-

---

13. M. Weinfeld, "Covenant Terminology in the Ancient Near East and Its Influence on the West," *Journal of the Oriental Society*, 93.2 (1973), 197.

cient world, is to be located in the profound influence of a single man—God's servant, Noah.

Of course covenants did not begin with Noah, even though the word "covenant" first appears in the flood narrative (Gen. 6:18). That the word "covenant" is not used in the creation account does not mean that "covenant" is irrelevant to creation. On the contrary, the very process of creation can only be described as a covenantal process. Simply stated, the creation as described in Genesis involved a fourfold process: God commands; creation obeys; God evaluates; God blesses. Creation by this sort of process means that the world comes into existence under God's authority in obedience to Him with His blessing. In a few words, that describes a covenant relationship.

Creation, Covenant, and God

The question is, why would God create the world by such a process? There are, presumably, an infinite number of different methods God could have used to create the world. Out of all of the many different possible ways, why create through a covenantal process? Is it perhaps that the account in Genesis is merely an accommodation? Are we to believe that God's revelation to Moses is given in covenantal language because Moses and the children of Israel would be better able to understand language that fit with the culture of their own day?

Something like this is often suggested. But if this were the case, it would mean that the act of creation, which the Bible in many places extols as wonderful revelation of God, would not be a revelation of God at all, except to say that He is the kind of God who accommodates Himself. He is willing to stoop down to Israel's level. Perhaps the heavens would still reveal the glory of God and the firmament show His handiwork, but we would not know much about the God behind it all if the covenantal revelation of Scripture does not show us who He is in Himself.

In other words, if God as He reveals Himself in the economy of creation and salvation were not the same God who exists from eternity in loving Trinitarian fellowship, we would have no knowledge of God. His revelation would not truly reveal Him. We would not know the God we trust in, pray to, and worship. What the Scripture shows us is that the God of the economy is distinctly and profoundly covenantal in all that He does—beginning with the very act of creation, and continuing from that time in every aspect of His historical relationship with man, through the saving works of the Son, to the final climax of redemption when the new heavens and the new earth descends. In all this, there is nothing that is not covenantal. Either this reveals the Father, Son, and Spirit, or we do not know God.

Since we do know God and we know that His word reveals who He is, the fact that in the economy He only acts and reveals in and through covenants does teach us about His own nature. He creates and redeems through covenants not because He is accommodating to our creaturely weakness or because there is no other way for Him to relate to creatures. Rather, His whole relationship with man, His image, reflects His own "internal structure." Father, Son, and Spirit, relate to one another in covenant. Therefore, man as God's image must be created in a covenantal environment as a covenantal being who will move through a covenantal history to a covenantal climax.

This leads us to a fuller and richer definition of a covenant grounded in the Triune God Himself. James B. Jordan offers the following: *"The covenant is a personal-structural bond which joins the three Persons of God in a community of life, and in which man was created to participate.*"[14]

In Jordan's definition, there are three aspects.[15] First, among the Persons of the Trinity, the covenant is a personal relationship of love. Second, the Persons of the Trinity are bound to one another. There is a "rule" among them according to which each Person acts according to who He is and in terms of which He respects the others. Third, the community of life which is the Trinity has a personal structure. The hierarchy of the Persons reflects the rule among them and finds its most concrete expression in the outworking of the love of the three.

To put this in other words, the Father, Son, and Spirit love one another perfectly, each denying Himself for the others, giving Himself wholly for the others, each seeking the others' glory and benefit above His own. But this love also has a specific structure because each person's love flows and works according to the nature of the person and His relationship to the other two persons. It is not the same for the Father to love the Son as it is for the Son to love the Father or for the Spirit to love the Son. The First Person is always first, the Second, second, the Third, third. Only the Father generates. Only the Son is begotten. Only the Spirit proceeds from the Father and the Son. Their mutual love operates in accordance to the distinctions of the persons.

This is not theological speculation. The distinct forms of love, mutual glorification, and self-sacrificial giving I refer to are all revealed aspects of the relationship between Father, Son, and Spirit, especially in the

---

14. James B. Jordan, *The Law of the Covenant* (Tyler, TX: Institute for Christian Economics, 1984), 5. Italics in the original.
15. Ibid, 7.

Gospel of John. For example, Jesus told the Jews that "the Father loves the Son, and shows Him all things that He Himself is doing" (5:20) and "I do nothing on My own initiative, but I speak these things as the Father taught Me" (8:28). The Father's love for the Son is revealed in that He shows and teaches the Son. The Son's love, however, is revealed in a manner that fits His place as Son, "If you keep My commandments, you will abide in My love; just as I have kept My Father's commandments and abide in His love" (15:10).

Theology of Father and Son and Deuteronomy

Suppose that we conclude that Father, Son, and Spirit relate to one another in covenant, that the three Persons of the Trinity create and save through covenants because of the kind of relationship they have among themselves. What does all of this have to do with Deuteronomy? There are at least four very clear implications for our understanding of Deuteronomy. First, the theology of the Trinitarian covenant provides the theological foundation for understanding the Father/son relationship between Yahweh and Israel, which is the heart and soul of Deuteronomy. Second, by doing so, it enables us to better see Israel's relationship to Yahweh in the whole flow of Biblical history. Third, by relating the Trinitarian covenant to the book of Deuteronomy, we obtain a new vista on the life of Christ, or at least a more concrete picture. Fourth, this perspective highlights the profound relevance of Deuteronomy for modern Christians. Let's consider each of these briefly.

First, consider how the theology of the Trinitarian covenant is important for Deuteronomy. To begin with, the same sorts of questions that we ask about creation can also be asked about the book of Deuteronomy. Of all the ways that Yahweh could have described His relationship to Israel in Deuteronomy, why should He describe it not only as a covenant, but as a Father/son relationship? The ultimate answer to this question suggested by what we have seen above is that the Father/son relationship between Yahweh and Israel reflects the Father/Son relationship between the eternal Father and Son.[16] The loving Yahweh instructs the son with commandments that show him the way of life and blessing, just as the Father teaches His Son Jesus all things. All of these commandments, therefore, show us who our God is and how He relates to His incarnate Son, Jesus.

Second, consider what this says about Israel. Though the theme is revealed in many ways and places, when we consider the larger theological context for the Father/son relationship between Yahweh and Israel, it is clear that Israel is a new Adam inasmuch as Israel's relationship with Yahweh is the same as Adam's original relationship. Luke specifically calls Adam a "son of God" (Luke 3:38), but the notion of Adam being created "in God's image" already implies sonship (cf. Gen. 5:3). Adam the son rebelled against the Father and was cast out of the home, but Yahweh always waited with long-

---

16. Frank Moore Cross points out that "The social organization of West Semitic tribal groups was grounded in kinship." He shows that other societies besides Israel regarded their gods as father or a kinsman. This is exactly what we should expect if ancient societies had historical roots in Noah and if his son Shem lived long after the tower of Babel. In the covenant relationship among the Persons of the Trinity and its reflection in God's relationship with man from Adam to Noah, the Bible offers us a theologically profound answer to the important historical question, why is covenantal thinking so widespread and so remarkably similar throughout the ancient world? Cross, *From Epic to Canon: History and Literature in Ancient Israel* (Baltimore: Johns Hopkins University Press, 2000), 3.

ing for His prodigal son to return. Even more in the sonship of Israel, Yahweh sought His son and pleaded with him through His servants the prophets.

But with the prophets the predominant metaphor changes. Ezekiel and Hosea, for example, picture Yahweh's relationship to His people primarily in terms of the analogy of marriage. Israel and Judah are depicted as Yahweh's bride; the husband/wife imagery dominates the prophets. Nevertheless Hosea can still say, "Out of Egypt I called My son" (11:1). It seems that the one metaphor does not rule out the other. In Deuteronomy, the law of the rebellious son, especially understood in the light of Adam and Christ, provides a perspective that illumines Israel's history all the way to the coming of the Messiah.

This brings us to our third point. Jesus' self-understanding is explicitly set forth in terms of the Father/son relationship in Deuteronomy. The Gospels of Matthew and Luke show us that immediately after Jesus' baptism, He went into the wilderness to be tempted by the devil and that the first temptation was to turn stones into bread. Jesus answered Satan by quoting from Deuteronomy 8:3, a passage speaking of Yahweh training His son Israel in the wilderness by letting him become hungry. In this quotation, Jesus reveals that He seems Himself as the fulfillment of the meaning of Israel. He is the true Son who will submit to and obey the Father and so fulfill the role for which Israel was elected. Each of the other temptations was also answered by a quotation from Deuteronomy, again emphasizing that Jesus saw Himself as the new Israel.

Ironically, Jesus alluded to the law of the rebellious son when He condemned the people of his generation who accused Him of being a glutton and a drunkard (Matt. 11:19; Luke 7:34). Jesus died the death of the rebellious son even though He was the only Israelite who ever honored the Father. The rebellious Jews of Jesus' day killed Him for rebelling against their authority and for not honoring them, though they had made God's word void through their traditions (Mark 7:6–13).

Furthermore, the commandments and instruction of Deuteronomy reveal to us the daily life of Jesus. Jesus Himself told us "And He who sent Me is with Me; He has not left Me alone, for I always do the things that are pleasing to Him" (8:29). We know the commandments Jesus obeyed and the things He did day by day because Deuteronomy, along with Exodus, Leviticus, and Numbers, teaches the way of Yahweh for His son Israel, the way which Jesus fulfilled. Jesus' concern for the poor, His compassion on the sinful, and even His indignation at the Pharisees' hypocrisy all find foundational forms in the instruction Moses gave to Israel in Deuteronomy.

Finally, if the book of Deuteronomy teaches us the commandments and instruction that Jesus obeyed as the perfect Son of the Father, it remains profoundly relevant for Christian ethics for it shows us how Christ lived. We are to walk in Jesus' ways and imitate Him (1 John 2:6). To be sure, we are not under the law as our covenant, as ancient Israel was. Its teaching applies to us less directly, but it applies all the same. And for most of her history, the church has seen the relevance of Deuteronomy not only for daily godliness, but also for political wisdom. This was especially true from the Reformation to early America.

> The use of Deuteronomy reached its apogee during the Protestant Reformation in the sixteenth and seventeenth centuries when the founders of the new Swiss, Huguenot, Rhineland, Dutch, Puritan, and Scottish commonwealths rested their polities on Deuteronomy as Israel's Ancient Deuteronomic

foundations. The culmination of this trend came at the time of the American revolutionary polemical literature between 1765 and 1805. As Donald Lutz has pointed out, Deuteronomy was cited more frequently than all citations of European political philosophers combined, a major source for the myriad political sermons of the period.[17]

Deuteronomy was the covenant of Yahweh with His son, the nation Israel, and it was given to the son to provide comprehensive guidance for life, political as well as religious and personal. Jesus fulfilled the meaning of Deuteronomy by keeping its commandments and taking on Himself the burdens of the law that Israel could not, including the burden of sin which He bore on the cross as the true Lamb of God. As we have seen, the Father/son covenant of Deuteronomy is grounded in the most profound teaching of the Bible, the Trinity, and has far-reaching significance for the Christian life. It deserves the devoted attention of modern Christians who seek to imitate the Son and please the Father through the Holy Spirit.

---

17. Daniel J. Elazar, "Deuteronomy as Israel's Ancient Constitution: Some Preliminary Reflections." Online at http://www.jcpa.org/dje/articles2/deut-const.htm

Conclusion

As this study shows, the heart of Deuteronomy is the love of Yahweh the Father for His wayward and foolish son Israel. Deuteronomy is instruction of grace, presupposing the Father/son relationship. There is nothing here like the sometimes-asserted "Covenant of Works"—do this and you will become a son. Sonship is a gift, even prior to the act of delivering Israel from Egypt (Ex. 4:22). The Exodus itself and the gift of the Mosaic covenant are extensions of the Abrahamic covenant and manifestations of the covenant love of Yahweh.

Though Israel was a rebellious son and though Moses prophesied that they would continue to be stiff-necked and stubborn, he also prophesied that the day would come when through discipline for their sin they would be led to true repentance and faith. Yahweh would not finally reject His son; He would redeem him. Thus, the law given to Israel in Deuteronomy was not primarily "law" in the way modern men think of it, though it remains true that Deuteronomy can be described as the constitution of ancient Israel. The Law of Moses was first of all—and primarily—fatherly instruction from Yahweh. That instruction included social, religious, and political dimensions because Yahweh's son was a nation that needed instruction in all these areas.

It is most profoundly significant that the instruction was given in the form of a covenant—a relationship which reflects the intra-Trinitarian love of Father, Son, and Spirit. Deuteronomy teaches modern Christians how to think about the kingdom Jesus came to establish, even though it is not a simple blueprint. We read Deuteronomy to know how Yahweh the Father instructed His immature child Israel (cf. Gal. 4:1–7), to know how Jesus obeyed the Father, and to understand the heart and will of our heavenly Father, so that we might be obedient sons who will inherit the blessings of the Fifth Word, to live long and be blessed in serving Jesus, our covenant Lord.

Appendix I

In this appendix, I list the various references to the Fifth Word, direct and indirect, in the order that they appear in Deuteronomy. I am not entirely satisfied with the format of my book because it takes the reader away from the impact that is derived from a straightforward reading of the text. I have included the context of the quotations in many instances, so to make the references clear, I put the crucial phrases in italics.

> Yahweh your God who goeth before you, he will fight for you, according to all that he did for you in Egypt before your eyes, and in the wilderness, where thou hast seen how that Yahweh thy God bare thee, *as a man doth bear his son,* in all the way that ye went, until ye came unto this place. (1:30–31)

> When thou shalt beget children, and children's children, and ye shall have been long in the land, and shall corrupt yourselves, and make a graven image in the form of anything, and shall do that which is evil in the sight of Yahweh thy God, to provoke

him to anger; I call heaven and earth to witness against you this day, that ye shall soon utterly perish from off the land whereunto ye go over the Jordan to possess it; *ye shall not prolong your days* upon it, but shall utterly be destroyed. (4:25–26)

Know therefore this day, and lay it to thy heart, that Yahweh he is God in heaven above and upon the earth beneath; there is none else. And thou shalt keep his statutes, and his commandments, which I command thee this day, that *it may go well* with thee, and with thy children after thee, and that thou mayest *prolong thy days* in the land, which Yahweh thy God giveth thee, for ever. (4:39–40)

Honor thy father and thy mother, as Yahweh thy God commanded thee; that thy days may be long, and that it may go well with thee, in the land which Yahweh thy God giveth thee. (5:16)

And Yahweh heard the voice of your words, when ye spake unto me; and Yahweh said unto me, I have heard the voice of the words of this people, which they have spoken unto thee: they have well said all that they have spoken. Oh that there were such a heart in them, that they would fear me, and keep all my commandments always, *that it might be well with them, and with their children for ever!* (5:28–29)

Ye shall walk in all the way which Yahweh your God hath commanded you, that ye may live, and that *it may be well* with you, and that *ye may prolong your days* in the land which ye shall possess. (5:33)

Now this is the commandment, the statutes, and the ordinances, which Yahweh your God commanded me to teach you, that ye might do them in the land whither ye go over to possess it; that thou mightest

Appendix I

fear Yahweh thy God, to keep all his statutes and his commandments, which I command thee, thou, and thy son, and thy son's son, all the days of thy life; and *that thy days may be prolonged*. Hear therefore, O Israel, and observe to do it; *that it may be well* with thee, and that ye may increase mightily, as Yahweh, the God of thy fathers, hath promised unto thee, in a land flowing with milk and honey. (6:1–3)

Ye shall not tempt Yahweh your God, as ye tempted him in Massah. Ye shall diligently keep the commandments of Yahweh your God, and his testimonies, and his statutes, which he hath commanded thee. And thou shalt do that which is right and good in the sight of Yahweh; *that it may be well* with thee, and that thou mayest go in and possess the good land which Yahweh sware unto thy fathers, to thrust out all thine enemies from before thee, as Yahweh hath spoken. (6:16–19)

And Yahweh commanded us to do all these statutes, to fear Yahweh our God, *for our good always*, that he might *preserve us alive*, as at this day. (6:24)

And thou shalt remember all the way which Yahweh thy God hath led thee these forty years in the wilderness, that he might humble thee, to prove thee, to know what was in thy heart, whether thou wouldest keep his commandments, or not. And he humbled thee, and suffered thee to hunger, and fed thee with manna, which thou knewest not, neither did thy fathers know; that he might make thee know that man doth not live by bread only, but by every word that proceedeth out of the mouth of Yahweh doth man live. Thy raiment waxed not old upon thee, neither did thy foot swell, these forty years. And thou shalt consider in thy heart, that, *as a man chasteneth his son*, so Yahweh thy God chasteneth thee. Therefore thou shalt keep the commandments of Yahweh thy God, to walk in his ways, and to fear him. (8:2-6)

. . . who fed thee in the wilderness with manna, which thy fathers knew not; that he might humble thee, and that he might prove thee, *to do thee good* at thy latter end. (8:16)

And now, Israel, what doth Yahweh thy God require of thee, but to fear Yahweh thy God, to walk in all his ways, and to love him, and to serve Yahweh thy God with all thy heart and with all thy soul, to keep the commandments of Yahweh, and his statutes, which I command thee this day *for thy good?* (10:12-13)

Therefore shall ye keep all the commandment which I command thee this day, that ye may be strong, and go in and possess the land, whither ye go over to possess it; and *that ye may prolong your days* in the land, which Yahweh sware unto your fathers to give unto them and to their seed, a land flowing with milk and honey. (11:8-9)

Therefore shall ye lay up these my words in your heart and in your soul; and ye shall bind them for a sign upon your hand, and they shall be for frontlets between your eyes. And ye shall teach them your children, talking of them, when thou sittest in thy house, and when thou walkest by the way, and when thou liest down, and when thou risest up. And thou shalt write them upon the door-posts of thy house, and upon thy gates; *that your days may be multiplied, and the days of your children,* in the land which Yahweh sware unto your fathers to give them, *as the days of the heavens above the earth.* (11:18-21)

Only be sure that thou eat not the blood: for the blood is the life; and thou shalt not eat the life with the flesh. Thou shalt not eat it; thou shalt pour it out upon the earth as water. Thou shalt not eat it; *that it may go well* with thee, and with *thy children after thee*, when thou shalt do that which is right in the eyes of Yahweh. (12:23–25)

Observe and hear all these words which I command thee, *that it may go well with thee*, and with *thy children after thee for ever*, when thou doest that which is good and right in the eyes of Yahweh thy God. (12:28)

Ye are the sons of Yahweh your God: ye shall not cut yourselves, nor make any baldness between your eyes for the dead. For thou art a holy people unto Yahweh thy God, and Yahweh hath chosen thee to be a people for his own possession, above all peoples that are upon the face of the earth. (14:1–2)

And it shall be, when he sitteth upon the throne of his kingdom, that he shall write him a copy of this law in a book, out of that which is before the priests the Levites: and it shall be with him, and he shall read therein all the days of his life; that he may learn to fear Yahweh his God, to keep all the words of this law and these statutes, to do them; that his heart be not lifted up above his brethren, and that he turn not aside from the commandment, to the right hand, or to the left: to the end *that he may prolong his days* in his kingdom, he and his children, in the midst of Israel. (17:18–20)

But if any man hate his neighbor, and lie in wait for him, and rise up against him, and smite him mortally so that he dieth, and he flee into one of these cities; then the elders of his city shall send and fetch him thence, and deliver him into the hand of the avenger of blood, that he may die. Thine eye shall not pity him, but thou shalt purge the innocent blood from Israel, *that it may go well* with thee. (19:11–13)

If a bird's nest chance to be before thee in the way, in any tree or on the ground, with young ones or eggs, and the dam sitting upon the young, or upon the eggs, thou shalt not take the dam with the young: thou shalt surely let the dam go, but the young thou mayest take unto thyself; *that it may be well* with thee, and that *thou mayest prolong thy days.* (22:6–7)

Thou shalt not have in thy bag diverse weights, a great and a small. Thou shalt not have in thy house diverse measures, a great and a small. A perfect and just weight shalt thou have; a perfect and just measure shalt thou have: *that thy days may be long* in the land which Yahweh thy God giveth thee. For all that do such things, even all that do unrighteously, are an abomination unto Yahweh thy God. (25:13–16)

And it shall come to pass, that, as Yahweh rejoiced over you *to do you good*, and to multiply you, so Yahweh will rejoice over you to cause you to perish, and to destroy you; and ye shall be plucked from off the land whither thou goest in to possess it. (28:63)

Yahweh thy God will bring thee into the land which thy fathers possessed, and thou shalt possess it; and *he will do thee good*, and multiply thee above thy fathers. (30:5)

See, I have set before thee this day *life and good*, and death and evil; in that I command thee this day to love Yahweh thy God, to walk in his ways, and to keep his commandments and his statutes and his ordinances, *that thou mayest live* and multiply, and that Yahweh thy God may bless thee in the land whither thou goest in to possess it. But if thy heart turn away, and thou wilt not hear, but shalt be drawn away, and worship other gods, and serve them; I denounce unto you this day, that ye shall surely perish; *ye shall not prolong your days* in the land, whither thou passest over the Jordan to go in to possess it. I call heaven and earth to witness against you this day, that *I have set before thee life* and death, the blessing and the curse: therefore *choose life, that thou mayest live, thou and thy seed*; to love Yahweh thy God, to obey his voice, and to cleave unto him; for he is thy life, and *the length of thy days*; that thou mayest dwell in the land which Yahweh sware unto thy fathers, to Abraham, to Isaac, and to Jacob, to give them. (30:15-20)

They have dealt corruptly with him,
They are not *his sons*,
It is their blemish;
They are a perverse and crooked generation.
Do ye thus requite Yahweh,
O foolish people and unwise?
Is not he thy father that hath bought thee?
He hath made thee, and established thee. (32:5-6)

You neglected *the Rock who begot you*,
And forgot *the God who gave you birth*.
And Yahweh saw it, and abhorred them,
Because of the provocation of *his sons and his
    daughters*.
And he said, I will hide my face from them,
I will see what their end shall be:
For they are a very perverse generation,
Sons in whom is no faithfulness. (32:18-20)

And Moses made an end of speaking all these words to all Israel. And he said unto them, Set your heart unto all the words which I testify unto you this day, which ye shall command your children to observe to do, even all the words of this law. For it is no vain word for you. Indeed *it is your life*. And by this word *ye shall prolong your days* in the land, whither ye go over the Jordan to possess it. (32:45–47)

Appendix II

New atheist leader Richard Dawkins takes devilish delight in slandering the name of Yahweh, the God of Israel.

> The God of the Old Testament is arguably the most unpleasant character in all fiction: jealous and proud of it; a petty, unjust, unforgiving control-freak; a vindictive, bloodthirsty ethnic cleanser; a misogynistic, homophobic, racist, infanticidal, genocidal, filicidal, pestilential, megalomaniacal, sadomasochistic, capriciously malevolent bully.[1]

Though certain elements of this list perhaps provide a classical illustration of the Freudian mechanism referred to as "projection," the entire list cannot be simply dismissed. There is much that Dawkins finds offensive about the "God of the Old Testament" which comes from the teaching of Deuteronomy. Though this

---

1. Richard Dawkins, *The God Delusion* (New York: Houghton Mifflin, 2006), 29.

list primarily represents a simple rejection of the possibility that Yahweh is the Creator, Dawkins' vilification of Yahweh also derives in part from a fundamental misreading of His relationship with Israel, a misreading that I suspect many Christians share to a degree, though they would not describe the "God of the Old Testament" as Dawkins has.

Of course, to say Yahweh is "homophobic" or "racist" or "genocidal" is simply to say that Yahweh is not God and therefore does not have the right to decide what is right and what is wrong, or to bring nations and peoples under judgment or into special favor. In other words, these accusations take a truth—that God condemns homosexuality, for example—and object to that teaching in language that is intentionally offensive. The charge of racism is a distorted representation of the fact that Yahweh did indeed choose Israel and did indeed also condemn certain peoples and nations to death. This is also the source of words like infanticidal, genocidal, filicidal, and the expression "bloodthirsty ethnic cleanser."

Now, if Yahweh were not God, megalomaniacal would be an appropriate adjective. There is much that He did and commanded that would invite moral condemnation—and not just from the perspective of a twenty-first-century, Christian-influenced atheist.[2] But if Yahweh is the Creator of the universe, we have to read His acts and words in a completely different light. In the nature of the case our judgments about what is right and wrong would have to be revised to fit with His. God condemns homosexuality in no uncertain

---

2. I never cease to be amused by atheists who believe that the universe is impersonal, but who nevertheless insist that we have a moral obligation to love one another. "Thou shalt love thy neighbor as the Big Bang loveth thee."

terms. That offends Dawkins and many others in our day. But when they reject their Creator's standards, it is not Him who is being unjust.

Which parts of the list come from a misreading of Yahweh's relationship with Israel? Consider the following items: jealous and proud of it, petty, unforgiving control-freak, capriciously malevolent bully. Again, if Yahweh were not the Creator, but a figment of Moses' imagination, we might object to what He said or did. But these accusations actually are not primarily denials that Yahweh is the Creator God. These are denials that He was a good Father to Israel. These terms from Dawkins dirty list pervert words and actions that display Yahweh's fatherhood.

Dawkins should be able to read the Old Testament differently. He is himself a husband, now with his third wife after two divorces, and a father. Now, when his daughter Juliet was a small child, I assume that Dawkins and his second wife, Eve, exercised considerable control over her. That is what parents do with small children. But we do not usually describe or think of them as "control freaks." Little children need to be protected, cared for, fed, and taught. When the book of Deuteronomy tells us that Yahweh carried the people of Israel through the wilderness as a father carries his child, it is giving us a perspective from which to understand the relationship. Just as fathers are not control freaks when they determine virtually everything for their two-year-old child, Yahweh was not a control freak in determining everything for ancient Israel.

Fathers delve into details of their children's lives in a way that might be petty if it were not a father/child relationship. A father may express his loving anger toward his child in a way that could be described as capricious bullying if that same anger were expressed to someone who was not his child. Whether or not the angry person is malevolent depends on who he is and what motivates his anger. When Yahweh is angry at Israel, He is angry as a father whose heart is broken because of the folly of His beloved son. His anger aims to save. Reading passages about God's anger as capricious bullying is quite the same as accusing a loving father of malevolent violence when he punishes his child in order to teach him not to play with fire.

I suspect there is another aspect of Dawkins' misreading, one that derives from a fundamental difference in modern ways of instruction, though again this relates to the father/child relationship. In the ancient world, most sons were taught their trade by their fathers. This would be especially true in the agricultural setting, but even in ancient cities and towns, it would have been usually the case also. Jesus, for example, almost certainly learned how to be a carpenter in his father's shop working by his side. When we remember that the father is a teacher, especially to the son, then certain aspects of Yahweh's relationship with Israel take on a different light.

> And thou shalt remember all the way which Jehovah thy God hath led thee these forty years in the wilderness, that he might humble thee, to prove thee, to know what was in thy heart, whether thou wouldest keep his commandments, or not. And he humbled thee, and suffered thee to hunger, and fed thee with manna, which thou knewest not, neither did thy fathers know; that he might make thee know that man doth not live by bread only, but by everything that proceedeth out of the mouth of Jehovah doth man live. Thy raiment waxed not old upon thee, neither did thy foot swell, these forty years. And thou shalt consider in thy heart, that, as a

man chasteneth his son, so Jehovah thy God chasteneth thee. (Deut. 8:2-5)

The father as teacher may well test his son. He may give him hard projects to complete or even say things intentionally problematic to provoke the right response from his son. All teachers test their students and good teachers find imaginative methods for motivating their students to think and grow.

Thus, Dawkins' calumny of the Biblical God is not only based on his hatred of the idea of a Creator, with all that it involves, but also on a perverse misreading of the God of Israel. God's loving care, His instruction, His passionate commitment to Israel are grotesquely distorted. Like the Pharisees hiding in the bushes waiting for Jesus to say or do anything they can turn against Him, Dawkins combs the Scriptures, reading every word through the jaundiced spectacles of skepticism, to find fault with Yahweh.

My own conclusion is that atheists like Dawkins and his fellow travelers Christopher Hitchens, Daniel Dennett, and Sam Harris are malevolent intellectual bullies, pushing their atheistic agenda as if it were the only intelligent option. These four "brights," as they hilariously call themselves, are arguably the most unpleasant characters in all pretended nonfiction.

www.ingramcontent.com/pod-product-compliance
Lightning Source LLC
Chambersburg PA
CBHW072053290426
44110CB00014B/1670